AT HOME AND AT LARGE
IN THE GREAT PLAINS

ESSAYS AND MEMORIES

PAUL A. JOHNSGARD

Upland sandpiper

At Home and at Large

in the Great Plains

Essays and Memories

Paul A. Johnsgard

Zea Books
Lincoln, Nebraska
2015

ISBN 978-1-60962-070-7   paperback
ISBN 978-1-60962-071-4   ebook

Set in Adobe Caslon types. Design and composition by
Paul Royster & Linnea Fredrickson.

Zea Books are published by
the University of Nebraska–Lincoln Libraries

Electronic (pdf) ebook edition available online at
http://digitalcommons.unl.edu/zeabook/

Print edition can be ordered from Lulu.com, at
http://www.lulu.com/spotlight/unllib

Contents

American bittern (p. 42)

Acknowledgments

This book would not and could not have been written if it were not for the existence of a local monthly newspaper called *Prairie Fire*. It is the brainchild of W. Don Nelson, who with his amazing crew of four elves have somehow miraculously managed to assemble and publish it nearly every month for seven years (as of 2015) and have arranged for its mostly free distribution across the better parts of the central Great Plains. It has carried important messages of social, environmental, and economic issues in a mature and nonpartisan manner to tens of thousands of residents of Nebraska, western Iowa, eastern Colorado, and southern South Dakota, and, by mail to subscribers, to the rest of our country. I have been privileged to write essays for *Prairie Fire* almost from its outset, and most of my thirty-plus essays have been republished elsewhere (in *Seasons of the Tallgrass Prairie* and *Natural Treasures of the Great Plains*). This volume includes fourteen of the remainder. *Prairie Fire*'s editor, Cris Trautner, has always kindly accepted every scrap of writing I have given her, and has even on occasion asked for more! I greatly appreciate the permission of *Prairie Fire* to reprint them here. All of the included essays were originally published in *Prairie Fire*, although some have been updated. Their original citations are at the end of the individual essays, and all my *Prairie Fire* essays are listed chronologically in my overall bibliography.

I have also included an updated version of an informal autobiography, written at the request of the Nebraska Ornithologists' Union and published in 2010 in the NOU journal, the *Nebraska Bird Review*. I owe the journal's editor, Janis Paseka, my sincere thanks for accepting and editing my earlier version, to which I have added a current list of all my published writings.

Finally, I must especially thank Dr. Paul Royster, coordinator of Scholarly Communications for the University of Nebraska–Lincoln Libraries and publisher of Zea Books. Without exception he has happily welcomed every published or unpublished manuscript I have thrown at him, even some that I probably would not have accepted if I were he. He has even diligently ferreted out and obtained permission to reproduce in the UNL Digital Commons some early publications that I had long since forgotten that I had ever written!

Sharp-tailed grouse

PART I

The Changing Bird Life
of the Great Plains

Western grebe

1

Nebraska: Where the West Begins
and the East Peters Out

In the mid-1800s, the immigrants following the North Platte River upstream knew they had finally entered the American West as they approached Chimney Rock, the most easterly of the iconic monoliths along the Oregon Trail. In the parlance of the day, this landmark, at longitude 103°20′W, confirmed that they were finally seeing the elephant. A general awareness that Nebraska represents a transition zone between East and West was formalized by the state legislature in 1963, in accepting our official state slogan as "Welcome to NEBRASKAland: Where the West Begins."

There is some biological evidence for this assertion. In 1887 Charles Bessey, botany professor at the University of Nebraska, reported finding a meeting place of eastern and western floras in western Rock County's Niobrara River valley, near the mouth of Long Pine Creek, at longitude 99°80′W. Roger T. Peterson vacillated in selecting the western terminus of coverage in early editions of his classic *A Field Guide to the Birds*, but by its fourth (1980) edition he had chosen the 100th meridian, the approximate longitudinal midpoint of the Great Plains. In a 1978 analysis of the zoogeography of more than two hundred species of breeding birds in the Great Plains, I also concluded that the 100th meridian represents a fairly accurate division point between eastern and western bird faunas, and also closely conforms to the middle of several hybrid zones that exist in several of the occasionally interbreeding species of Great Plains birds.

It is convenient to use conspicuous typical plants or plant communities in judging biogeographic classifications, as evidence of definable and climatically based biological units. For example, we think of characteristic shortgrass plains species (such as buffalo grass and big sagebrush), and comparable coniferous forest species (such as ponderosa and limber pines), as reliable indicator species of the American West. Similarly, characteristic plants of the tallgrass prairies (such as big bluestem and Indian grass) and deciduous forests (various oaks and maples) are easily recognizable species that are largely limited to eastern North America.

For example, in Nebraska there are six native eastern oak species, only two of which extend beyond the relatively moist Missouri River valley of extreme southeastern Nebraska. The red oak ranges north along this well-timbered valley to Dakota County and west along the Platte River valley to Saunders County. However, the much more drought- and fire-tolerant bur oak occurs west along the Niobrara valley to Dawes County, and along the Platte valley it ranges west to Custer County. Among the maples, the moisture-loving eastern silver maple is native to riverine forests over only the eastern third of the state. In contrast, the shrub-sized and relatively arid-adapted Rocky Mountain maple barely enters the state, eking out a marginal existence in the shady canyons of Sioux County.

Similarly, big sagebrush, which probably once occupied a million or more square miles in the Old West, occurs in northwestern Nebraska only in Sioux, Dawes, and Sheridan Counties. Among the western conifers, the arid- and timberline-adapted limber pine barely reaches southwestern Nebraska in Kimball County. However, the highly adaptable ponderosa pine penetrates east along the Niobrara valley to Keya Paha and Rock Counties, which was one of the reasons Charles Bessey selected Rock County as an important east-west floral transition zone.

It might be impossible to define precisely the meeting point of East and West over the broad geographic, climatic, and biological gradients that exist in the Great Plains. However, there are many interesting biological situations that arise in locations where two closely related western- and eastern-oriented species meet and interact. These conditions present probabilities of overlapping ecological niches and strong interspecies competition for the same environmental conditions as well as possibilities of interspecies hybridization.

For example, the Rocky Mountain juniper extends from Nebraska's western border counties east to Cherry County. Over part of its western Nebraska range this shrubland-adapted juniper is in contact with the more widespread and less drought-tolerant eastern red-cedar, and the two freely hybridize. For very closely related species such as these junipers, hybridization might not be harmful, and conceivably might even be beneficial if the two species are able to exchange their most desirable genes. But, the more distantly related two hybridizing species are, the less likely their two gene complexes can interact successfully, and the more probable that the resulting hybrids will be ill-adapted to the environment and unable to breed successfully. Over time, such coexisting species ultimately evolve sufficient genetically based differences as are needed to prevent crossbreeding.

While expanding their ranges, plants and animals often travel via convenient natural corridors, along which they can survive, reproduce, and disseminate progeny into new areas of dispersal. In Nebraska, the primary north-south wooded corridor has probably been the Missouri River. Strongly forest-dependent birds—such as the blue-gray gnatcatcher, eastern whip-poor-will, chuck-will's-widow, and pileated woodpecker—are examples of eastern forest-breeding birds that have been expanding northward along this narrow riparian corridor during historic times.

Likewise, breeding by other eastern birds—such as the Acadian flycatcher; Kentucky, prothonotary, and yellow-throated warblers; Louisiana waterthrush; summer tanager; and tufted titmouse—is now mostly limited in Nebraska to the mature, usually moist, forests of its central and southern Missouri valley. These species have shown little, if any, apparent recent breeding expansions, probably because of having specific niche requirements not easily found elsewhere.

Among plants, there are similarly many characteristic Missouri valley species that probably are unable to adapt and expand into the nearby upland forests, including trees such as the American hazel, bitternut and shagbark hickories, black cherry, ironwood, pawpaw, and rock elm. Some of the many forbs with similarly restricted Missouri valley distributions include the gray-headed coneflower, Indian-pipe, late boneset, pale touch-me-not, showy and yellow orchids, smooth blue and willow asters, Turk's-cap lily, and wild columbine.

Nebraska has several major river valleys, notably the Niobrara, Platte, and Republican, which offer opportunities for east-west riverine corridor movements. Considering only woodland or woodland-edge species, the American redstart and black-and-white warblers, ovenbird, and red-breasted nuthatch are largely restricted along the Niobrara River to a narrow east-west corridor. The limited availability of coniferous habitats may prevent the nuthatch from any future range expansion any farther east, just as limits on fairly cool and shady deciduous canopies may prevent the two warblers from extending much farther west.

Many of Nebraska's woodland songbirds have similar strong distributional affinities with both the Platte and Niobrara Rivers. Those species that are rather loosely dependent on a well-wooded corridor and that can also use smaller riparian and nonriparian woody habitats for breeding are most widespread and most common. Several examples of these include species-pairs, having both eastern and western relatives whose ranges were split during late glacial times, as tundra and grasslands expanded over the Great Plains. As wooded corridors across the plains have recently matured in the absence of frequent prairie fires, these species' expanding ranges have increasingly approached one another, and now many of them are in geographic and social contact.

Four major species-pairs with interacting western and eastern counterpart birds (the western forms listed first) are the Bullock's and Baltimore orioles, the lazuli and indigo buntings, the black-headed and rose-breasted grosbeaks, and the spotted and eastern towhees. The common ancestral populations of all these species-pairs were probably separated into western and eastern isolates during late Pleistocene times, and it is only recently that climatic and ecological changes have brought them together. In areas where these species geograph-ically overlap, the presence of mixed matings and occasional hybrids is of great interest to biologists.

Depending on the incidence of hybridization, and the relative re-productive fitness of hybrid offspring, it is possible to judge the degree of evolutionary divergence between the parental stock. If the hybrids are unable or less likely to reproduce, putting them at a disadvantage with nonhybrids, the two parental populations are best considered as genetically isolated species. Such is the case with all eight of the bird species just mentioned. In contrast, the red-shafted (western) and yellow-shafted (eastern) populations of the northern flicker have also come into relatively recent broad contact across much of Nebraska and elsewhere in the Great Plains. There they have thoroughly inter-bred, producing a variety of intergrades and blurring their genetic dif-ferences to the point that they are now classified as a single species.

During the current trend toward global warming, plant and an-imal ranges will continue to change, and extinctions of some species might occur. Bird species that have recently expanded into Nebraska from the south include the glossy ibis, cattle egret, white-winged dove, Eurasian collared-dove, and great-tailed grackle. Some tropical spe-cies that are now appearing in small but increasing numbers include the black-bellied whistling-duck, Neotropic cormorant, and Inca dove. Additionally, several birds that once regularly overwintered in Ne-braska, such as the Bohemian waxwing and snow bunting, now in-creasingly winter farther north.

In the central Great Plains, we can anticipate that a progressively warmer and drier climate will develop, unless effective international controls on carbon consumption are adopted. In Nebraska, we can also expect more recurrent droughts and reduced water availability, through excessive drawdowns of our aquifers and declining surface waters. Thus, in the near future, homeowners should plant buffalo grass rather than Kentucky bluegrass, and yuccas rather than roses. When planting trees, drought-tolerant species, such as bur oaks, are far better choices than more thirsty species, such as maples. Nebraskans should also not

15

be surprised to encounter armadillos in their backyards and someday might begin seeing black vultures overhead as a somber harbinger of hotter and drier days ahead.

References

Bessey, C. E. 1887. A meeting place of two floras. *Bulletin of the Torrey Botanical Club* 14:189–191.

Johnsgard, P. A. 2010. The drums of April. *Prairie Fire*, April 2010, pp. 12–13. http://www.prairiefirenewspaper.com/2010/04/the-drums-of-april

Johnsgard, P. A. 2015. *Global Warming and Population Responses among Great Plains Birds.* University of Nebraska–Lincoln DigitalCommons. 384 pp. http://digitalcommons.unl.edu/zeabook/. Print edition available from http://www.lulu.com/shop/http://www.lulu.com/shop/paul-johnsgard/global-warming-and-population-responses-among-great-plains-birds/paperback/product-22063416.html.

Kaul, R., D. Sutherland, and S. Rolfsmeier. 2006. *The Flora of Nebraska.* Lincoln: School of Natural Resources, University of Nebraska–Lincoln.

2

The Wings of March

For naturalists, March is a time for rejoicing, for on its soothing south winds sweep wave after wave of northbound migrant birds. By the first of March, the Platte River has usually fully thawed, although thin ice shelves might line its edges on frosty mornings, and dying snow patches are usually confined to deeper ditches and the shady sides of buildings.

Meadowlarks are appearing on fence posts along country roads and are tentatively starting to reclaim old territories or establish new ones. In towns and cities, cardinals have already been singing enthusiastically from trees and shrubs for nearly two months. Northbound sparrows and horned larks are now abandoning their winter foraging grounds in weedy edges, stubble, and plowed fields, and are disappearing from view, only to be replaced by countless red-winged blackbirds, whose loose flocks dance over the fields like restless spirits, searching for brief resting places.

Early March is a time in Nebraska when the natural world changes on an almost day-to-day basis, with spring arriving in erratic fits and starts, as bone-chilling north and welcome south winds blow across the plains in regular alternation. Nevertheless, day lengths during early March are increasing at a perceptible rate, and the sunrises and sunsets creep ever closer toward marking exact eastern and western compass points on the horizon.

As recently as forty years ago, the first of March represented the average arrival date for sandhill cranes at the Platte River. Recent warmer winters and earlier thaws have tended to shift their first arrival date back into mid-February, the birds being driven ever northward by a combination of hormones, experience, and melting ice. Thus, by the middle of February a few flocks of cranes are now usually braving the possibility of late blizzards and icy Platte River waters, giving them early opportunities at the waste grain scattered across the harvested cornfields of the Platte valley, from Grand Island west to Scottsbluff. During a few recent mild winters, a thousand or more have even overwintered along the Platte. Those cranes stopping on the Platte's eastern reaches are mostly headed for breeding areas in northeastern Canada, while the westernmost flocks staging along the North Platte River are headed to western Alaska and Siberia, as far as three thousand to four thousand miles distant.

The sandhill cranes arrive in the Platte valley none too soon. By the time they arrive, a million or more cold-tolerant snow geese are already present, and thousands of overwintering Canada geese are harvesting corn from fields all along the central and western Platte valley. Overwintering by Canada geese in the Platte valley has greatly increased in recent decades, so that tens of thousands of birds now often sit out the winter there, rather than pushing farther south. The snow goose flocks that now number roughly two million to three million and that once migrated northward along the Missouri valley have shifted westward to the Platte valley during the past few decades, perhaps because of greater foraging opportunities there. Scattered among the snow geese, and composing about 2 percent of the flocks, are nearly identical Ross's geese, miniature versions of snow geese that are also headed toward high-arctic nesting grounds.

Add to these multitudes the tens of thousands of cackling geese and the even larger numbers of greater white-fronted geese staging in the Platte, and the March goose population in the Platte valley and adjoining Rainwater Basin to the south may easily approach three million birds. And, adding to the mix, mallards and northern pintails are the vanguards of a dozen or more species of ducks that pour into the Platte valley and Rainwater Basin during early March. All in all, it is an avian spectacle possibly unmatched anywhere in North America, with perhaps ten million waterfowl and half a million sandhill cranes concentrating in the Platte valley at peak numbers.

And, if rarity rather than uncountable numbers is the naturalist's goal, then the possibility also exists of seeing a few whooping cranes, one of North America's rarest and most beautiful birds. Probably all of the historical Great Plains flock of whooping cranes, which now numbers nearly three hundred birds, pass through Nebraska each spring; however, whooping cranes tend to arrive later in spring than do the sandhill cranes, and very few are likely to appear before the first of April. They also migrate in small, family-sized groups, and, to avoid unnecessary (and highly illegal) disturbance and harassment, their exact stopping points are never publicized by state and federal agencies. As a result, it takes great luck to encounter any whooping cranes in the state.

Even more rare than whooping cranes are the "common" cranes of Eurasia, which have been reported in North America less than a dozen times. Most of these sightings have occurred in the Platte valley, where the birds have unexpectedly appeared among flocks of sandhill cranes. Probably these birds headed east rather than turning south upon reaching the Bering Strait during fall migration out of Siberia and followed sandhill cranes to their Great Plains wintering areas.

Unlike waterfowl and songbirds, which often migrate at night, cranes are daylight migrants, mainly because they rely on soaring ability to carry them from point to point. By using thermal updrafts, which develop during warm days as sun-warmed air rises up from the ground, the birds can ascend thousands of feet with little physical effort, and then glide on a slight downward flight path for many miles, until they locate another thermal.

At a flight speed of forty-five to fifty miles per hour, sandhill cranes can cover up to five hundred miles in a single ten-hour day, or nearly all the way from their Texas and New Mexico wintering grounds to the Platte valley. It is a great joy to be watching and waiting along the Platte after a warm March day and hear the clarion calls of arriving cranes thousands of feet above, as they recognize their long-remembered roosting sites of the Platte and begin a lazy circling glide downward to land among its protective sandbars and islands.

For the sandhill cranes, the Platte River offers safe nighttime roosting sites on sandy islands and bars sufficiently far from shore that coyotes or other land mammals can't reach them without wading through water and alerting the birds to possible danger. During the daylight hours, from about sunrise until sunset, the birds spend their time in harvested cornfields and wet meadows, eating predominantly corn, which is rapidly converted to fat stores needed for completing the long migration to arctic tundra. A small percentage of their Platte valley food consists of various invertebrates, such as snails and earthworms, providing the protein and calcium that will be needed for egg-laying and other aspects of reproduction.

The middle of March is the peak of goose migration in the Platte valley, with the goose population at or slightly past its peak, and the sandhill crane migration nearing its peak. This is the ideal time for venturing to the Platte valley between Grand Island and Kearney, the focal point of goose and crane concentrations. There, one might arrange to observe the dawn and dusk flights out of and back into the river roosts by the sandhill cranes in the comfort of riverside blinds, such as those provided by Audubon's Lillian Annette Rowe Sanctuary near Gibbon (308-468-5282). One might also watch from free public viewing platforms situated along the river at bridges south of Alda and Gibbon (off I-80 exits 305 and 285), or from the hike-bike bridge over the Platte at Fort Kearny State Recreation Area (off I-80 exit 272).

During the day motorists may watch cranes and geese feeding in fields near the river (by driving country roads such as the Platte River Road from Doniphan west) and revel in the countless skeins of geese and ducks passing overhead, spread out from horizon to horizon, like animated strings of Christmas decorations. Avoid leaving the car and flushing the flocks during these times, as it not only needlessly disturbs the birds but also robs them of the precious foraging time they must have for replenishing their energy stores.

In recent years perhaps twenty thousand to thirty thousand people have annually made trips to the Platte valley in March to witness this unique spectacle, and I have personally accompanied visitors from as far away as Europe, Pakistan, and Japan. To do so is to provide a gift easily given, and one that I know they will carry in their memories and cherish for a lifetime. It is also a gift that all Nebraskans who love the natural world should consider giving themselves.

Spring Bird Migrations in Nebraska

Sandhill cranes. Sandhill cranes begin arriving in the Platte valley, usually reaching a peak about March 20. Some remain until about April 20. By far the best places to observe dawn and dusk roosting flights are at the blinds operated by Rowe Sanctuary (308-468-5282) and the Crane Trust (308-382-1820). Otherwise, the bridges south of Alda and Gibbon offer the best public viewing. Daytime viewing is best along the Platte River Road from Doniphan west to the Kearney area.

Whooping cranes. Far less predictable than sandhills, lone whooping cranes sometimes arrive with early-arriving sandhills, but family groups usually arrive April 1–15 and remain no more than a few days. Their daytime foraging is done on rather isolated and larger wetlands in the Rainwater Basin, and news of their whereabouts while they are here is quite restricted to avoid harassment.

Geese. Large forms of Canada geese overwinter along the Platte valley, while cackling, snow, Ross's, and greater white-fronted usually have arrived by March 1 and peak by mid-March. At least during wet springs, the larger marshes in the Rainwater Basin hold the largest numbers, but in dry years only a few basins that are provided with supplemental water will attract them. The arctic-breeding geese are largely gone by the end of March.

Ducks. Mallards, northern pintails, and common mergansers overwinter along the Platte, while most of another twenty-plus duck species arrive during March. Mallards and pintails peak with the arctic geese and tend to leave at the same time. Late-arriving ducks, such as ruddy ducks and blue-winged teal, may peak in early April, and ruddy ducks may not begin pairing displays until May. Sand-hills marshes, such as at Crescent Lake National Wildlife Refuge (NWR), are best for observing most ducks, especially the breeding species.

Pelicans. American white pelicans can be seen in small numbers on the Platte River, but the larger reservoirs, such as Harlan County, Calamus, and Lake McConaughy, hold the largest number—usually several hundreds. Their numbers peak from late March through April. Some nonbreeders remain in the state through summer.

Shorebirds. Shorebird migration in Nebraska is dispersed geographically and temporally but tends to peak in early May. Some larger species, such as long-billed curlews, begin to appear in April. The Sandhills marshes are especially good for American avocets, Wilson's phalaropes, and typical sandpipers, but in wet springs the Rainwater Basin may hold vast numbers of shorebirds. Probably the most sought after and hardest to find shorebird is the rare buff-breasted sandpiper, which is mostly found in stubble fields east of York. It usually forages in small flocks, often in association with golden or black-bellied plovers.

Eagles. Bald eagles are residents along all of Nebraska's rivers, but in winter and early spring they are most common around deep, open-water reservoirs, foraging on fish. Lake McConaughy holds the largest numbers, and an eagle-viewing building is open at Kingsley Dam during winter. In spring, their diet shifts to waterfowl, and they gather wherever large numbers of geese are found. Like arctic geese, bald eagles move northward as wetlands farther north become ice free. Golden eagles are too rare in Nebraska to offer reliable viewing locations, but shortgrass areas with bluffs and rim-rock exposures in the Pine Ridge region are the most likely places to search.

Prairie grouse. Both sharp-tailed grouse and greater prairie-chickens can be found in the central and eastern Sandhills, and both species primarily display throughout April, peaking around the middle of the month and ending by mid-May. Using a professional guide is the best choice for people with limited time schedules, but free first-come access to permanent sharp-tail blinds is available at the Bessey Division of the Nebraska National Forest near Halsey.

Favorite Spring Birding Locations in the Great Plains

For Nebraskans, trying to decide where to go birding in the spring is like trying to decide between chocolate and strawberry ice cream. The Platte valley, with its amazing numbers of cranes and waterfowl, is virtually my second home during March, but that has not prevented occasional trips to other locations having other attractions. Over the years I have made birding trips to nearly all the great birding places of the Great Plains between North Dakota and Oklahoma, with occasional forays beyond. Here, I suggest several of my favorite sites, choosing one each for Nebraska and four of its adjoining states. All five sites are within four hundred miles of Lincoln or Omaha, and nearly all (with one exception) have the highest published number of spring bird species so far reported for any location in that state. All are national wildlife refuges, having (with one exception) free public access, and all have seasonally specific bird lists. All have headquarters that provide toilet facilities and varying degrees of information on the natural history and biological diversity of the site. Numbers of bird species mentioned below are based on the most recent information that I have, but some are no doubt out of date by now, and the totals should be considered as minimums.

Nebraska

Crescent Lake National Wildlife Refuge is the largest of any of the sites described here (45,818 acres) and is easily the most remote. It is located about twenty-five miles north of Oshkosh, in the heart of the nineteen-thousand-square-mile Nebraska Sandhills. The road from Oshkosh is poor but is of near-interstate quality compared to roads on the refuge itself. One should leave Oshkosh with a full gas tank and carry both food and water; the only toilet on the refuge is located at the small headquarters building. The sand roads on the refuge can seem like quicksand in wet weather, and even under ideal conditions, one should try to park on the level or a downhill slope and on a grassy site rather than bare sand. Yet, with these simple precautions in mind, there should be no problems, and a visitor will soon discover why this is my favorite of all Nebraska's national wildlife refuges. The great Ogallala Aquifer lies just below the base of the Sandhills here, so dozens of shallow marshes and lakes are present. These wetlands vary from slightly alkaline to highly alkaline, the former used by two dozen species of waterfowl and the latter attracting a separate and distinct array of birds, such as the American avocet, black-necked stilt, Wilson's phalarope, and other shorebirds.

A total of 248 species have been reported on the refuge during spring, 12 of which are classified as abundant. Several of these are waterfowl (northern pintail, blue-winged teal, and northern shoveler), but they also include shorebirds such as the killdeer and Wilson's phalarope. Other abundant spring birds are the mourning dove, barn swallow, marsh wren, common yellowthroat, grasshopper sparrow, red-winged blackbird, western meadowlark, and yellow-headed blackbird. Crescent Lake is a great place for watching western and eared grebes in spring display, and sharp-tailed grouse are in peak display during April. Camping on the refuge isn't permitted, so seeing grouse display is difficult, but they are often visible along roadsides. Golden eagles and peregrine falcons are fairly rare, but I have seen them several times in spring, and seeing burrowing owls and long-billed curlews is relatively feasible during late April and May. American bitterns and black-crowned night-herons are fairly easily found, and white-faced ibises are also good possibilities.

Iowa

DeSoto National Wildlife Refuge lies along the banks of the Missouri River and is partly located in Nebraska. It consists of 7,823 acres and can be reached by driving five miles east of Blair, Nebraska. Besides the river-bottom habitat, there is a 750-acre oxbow lake, with a modern visitor center at one end. Unlike the other sites described here, Desoto NWR charges a small daily admission fee and has slightly fewer reported bird species (240) than does the Upper Mississippi River NWR, at the eastern end of the state. Yet, 187 species are present on DeSoto's spring bird list, including five that are classified as abundant. One of these (the snow goose) no longer occurs in large numbers during spring, but other abundant spring species are the mallard, ring-necked pheasant, mourning dove, and red-winged blackbird. One of DeSoto's unique features is an extensive exhibit of artifacts recovered from a sunken paddle-wheel ship of the mid-1800s, the *Bertrand.* These materials, mostly items that had been on their way to silver mining camps in Montana, provide a fascinating look at life during the middle of the nineteenth century. DeSoto NWR has a good deal of riparian and bottomland woods that make for fine spring birding; twenty-one species of warblers are on the spring list, and at least four (yellow, black-and-white, American redstart, and common yellowthroat) have been reported to nest.

Missouri

Squaw Creek National Wildlife Refuge lies about five miles south of Mound City in northwestern Missouri. Its 6,919 acres lie just east of the Missouri River, in rich prairie bottomland, and include a shallow marsh fed by two small creeks. The refuge's bird list includes 277 total species, with more than 100 nesting species and a spring list of 264 species. Beyond this very high overall spring diversity, 12 species are listed as abundant during spring. These include often phenomenally large flocks of snow geese (a million or more birds have been reported in some years). Other abundant spring birds include the Canada goose, mallard, northern pintail, American coot, bank swallow, red-winged blackbird, and brown-headed cowbird. Large numbers of bald eagles overwinter and remain until the great snow goose flocks depart in March. Hundreds of trumpeter swans also overwinter, and many of these spectacular birds remain well into spring. At least two pairs of sandhill cranes have nested on the refuge in recent years (providing Missouri's first modern breeding records for this species) and have either overwintered locally or returned very early in the spring.

Kansas

Quivira National Wildlife Refuge, named for the mythical city of gold unsuccessfully searched for by early Spanish explorers, is nevertheless very real and is an ornithological gold mine. Located in central Kansas about ten miles south of Ellinwood along Rattlesnake Creek, its 21,820 acres consist of two large salt marshes fed by a system of dikes and canals that result in about 5,000 acres of shallow wetlands. These wetlands are major spring staging areas for two hundred thousand waterfowl, plus thousands of American white pelicans and sandhill cranes, and have been designated as critical habitat for whooping cranes. The site's total list of 344 species is the largest of any of the sites described here, and its spring bird list of 267 species is also the largest seasonal list. Species that have in the past been classified as abundant during spring include the American white pelican; greater white-fronted and Canada geese; green-winged and blue-winged teal; mallard; northern pintail; northern shoveler; gadwall; American wigeon; redhead; lesser scaup; American kestrel; ring-necked pheasant; sandhill crane; lesser yellowlegs; white-rumped sandpiper; Baird's sandpiper; Wilson's phalarope; Franklin's gull; mourning dove; bank, barn, cliff, and northern rough-winged swallows; American crow; American robin; yellow-rumped warbler; red-winged blackbird; and western meadowlark. Some of the rare spring birds that remain to nest include the least tern, snowy plover, American avocet, black-necked stilt, and white-faced ibis. It is much harder to find the black, king, and Virginia rails and the common moorhen.

South Dakota

Lacreek National Wildlife Refuge lies close to the Nebraska border in the northern Sandhills region, about thirteen miles southeast of Martin. It consists of 16,420 acres, including 5,000 acres of impounded marshes surrounded by native sandhills prairie. The refuge and its bird life closely resemble Crescent Lake NWR. Its bird list consists of 281 species, of which 246 have been reported during spring. Twenty-two species have been classified in the past as abundant during spring, including the American white pelican, double-crested cormorant, snow and Canada geese, mallard, northern pintail, blue-winged teal, gadwall, ring-necked pheasant, killdeer, mourning dove, eastern and western kingbirds, horned lark, marsh wren, yellow warbler, common yellowthroat, lark bunting, red-winged blackbird, western meadowlark, and yellow-headed blackbird. Trumpeter swans and American white pelicans breed here, the swans overwintering and the pelicans likely to be present by the end of March. Western grebes arrive fairly early in spring and breed here, as do American bitterns, black-crowned night herons, long-billed curlews, and Forster's terns.

References

Brown, M. B., and P. A. Johnsgard. 2013. *Birds of the Central Platte River Valley and Adjacent Counties*. Lincoln: Zea Books and University of Nebraska–Lincoln DigitalCommons, http://digitalcommons.unl.edu/zeabook/15/. 182 pp. Print edition available from http://www.lulu.com/shop/paul-a-johnsgard-and-mary-bomberger-brown/.

Canterbury, J. L., P. A. Johnsgard, and H. F. Downing. 2013. *Birds and Birding in Wyoming's Bighorn Mountains Region*. Lincoln: Zea Books and University of Nebraska–Lincoln DigitalCommons. http://digitalcommons.unl.edu/zeabook/18/. 260 pp. Print edition available from http://www.lulu.com/shop/paul-a-johnsgard-and-jacqueline-l-canterbury-and-helen-f-downing/birds-and-birding-in-wyomings-bighorn-mountains-region/paperback/product-21777223.html.

Johnsgard, P. A. 2009. The wings of March. *Prairie Fire*, March 2009, pp. 1, 17, 18, 19. http://www.prairiefirenewspaper.com/2009/03/nature-notes-wings-of-march

Johnsgard, P. A. 2011. *A Nebraska Bird-Finding Guide*. Lincoln: Zea Books and University of Nebraska–Lincoln DigitalCommons. http://digitalcommons.unl.edu/zeabook/5/. 166 pp. Print edition available from http://www.lulu.com/shop/paul-johnsgard/.

Johnsgard, P. A. 2012. *Wetland Birds of the Central Plains: South Dakota, Nebraska, and Kansas*. Lincoln: Zea Books and University of Nebraska–Lincoln DigitalCommons http://digitalcommons.unl.edu/zeabook/8/. 275 pp. Print edition available from http://www.lulu.com/shop/paul-johnsgard/.

Johnsgard, P. A. 2013. *The Birds of Nebraska*. Rev. ed. Lincoln: Zea Books and University of Nebraska–Lincoln DigitalCommons, http://www.digitalcommons.unl.edu/zeabook/17/. ca. 150 pp. Print edition available from http://www.lulu.com/shop/paul-johnsgard/the-birds-of-nebraska-revised-edition-2013/paperback/product-21096798.html.

3

The Bird-feeder Birds of Nebraska

Feeding and watching wild birds at a feeding station is one of the most pleasant ways of spending time during Nebraska's long and dreary winter period. It has become a multimillion-dollar business, and recreational bird-feeding now involves almost one-third of all adult North Americans, or about the combined total of Americans regularly engaged in hunting and fishing. Not only does it provide unlimited entertainment, but it can be a wonderful way to learn to identify many of our native birds, often closer than would be possible by simply trying to observe them in the wild.

Of Nebraska's roughly 350 species of regularly occurring birds, about 100 are likely to be seen during the winter period. The most recent Nebraska winter survey available, the 2012 Great Backyard Bird Count, tallied 104 species. This count totaled more than 114,000 birds from more than 800 locations in Nebraska. Besides typical bird-feeder species, 21 species of ducks, geese, and swans and 15 species of raptors were also reported. However, nearly half of the species observed were those that might be seen at or at least near a typical urban or suburban Nebraska backyard feeding station. Among the typical bird-feeder species seen, the 11 most abundant, in descending sequence, were American goldfinch, dark-eyed junco, European starling, house sparrow, American robin, rock pigeon, house finch, northern cardinal, American tree sparrow, American crow, and black-capped chickadee.

In a comprehensive nationwide study of bird species likely to be seen at North American feeding stations, Erica Dunn and Diane Tessaglia-Hymes (1999) found that about 90 species regularly visit bird feeders and another 180 are casual visitors. Of the total that they identified as "regulars," about 40 species are common in Nebraska during winter. This list excludes various raptors that are attracted to prey at feeders and several game birds, such as the ring-necked pheasant, northern bobwhite, and wild turkey, which sometimes are attracted to farmyards. The list does include 3 doves and pigeons, 5 woodpeckers, and 33 true songbirds. The majority of these species are basically seed eaters, but some are omnivore-scavengers (for example, crow, jay, magpie, starling), some are attracted to high-protein foods such as suet (woodpeckers, brown creeper, kinglets), and a few are adapted to fruit or berry eating during winter (waxwing, robin, bluebirds).

In a study that I performed during the 1990s that analyzed historic Christmas Bird Count data, I compared more than fifty years of counts from the Lincoln, Nebraska, area with comparable counts from Scottsbluff, Nebraska. This study revealed some substantial differences in species composition among birds having eastern versus western geographic affinities across the four-hundred-mile distance that separates the two cities. Eleven species with largely eastern geographic affinities were present during the Lincoln counts but were lacking from Scottsbluff's, while two species (mountain chickadee and evening grosbeak) were observed only at Scottsbluff. The Eurasian collared-dove was not seen at either location until after my analysis; this self-introduced and rapidly expanding species first appeared in Nebraska during the late 1990s and has since been reported from all of the state's ninety-three counties. Another expanding species, the house finch, has long had a resident population in western Nebraska but did not reach the Lincoln-Omaha area until the late 1980s. House finches are still increasing nationally and now often equal or exceed house sparrows at bird feeders, whereas the house sparrow has been in a slow but persistent national decline for several decades.

Each of the species that was reported has a variable degree of association with bird feeders, and in some cases, such as with the northern cardinal, it is likely that the species' northern and westward range expansion in the state has been significantly aided by bird-feeding activities. Additionally, winters have become significantly milder since the 1960s across the Great Plains, which has made overwintering survival less stressful for many species, allowing them to winter at more northerly latitudes (Johnsgard, 2009).

Of the three doves and pigeons listed, the introduced rock pigeon is mostly a bird associated with barnyards, elevators, or other places where waste grain is likely to be found, and until the 1960s it was ignored by the National Audubon Society when compiling Christmas Count data. During the 2011–12 counts, it was seen in all fifteen count locations, with about 4,700 birds tallied, while the Eurasian collared-dove was seen in fourteen locations, with 811 birds tallied. Mourning doves tend to leave Nebraska during severe winters, but during the 2011–12 counts, nearly 400 were seen in nine locations. They come readily to feeders and are especially fond of smaller items, such as cracked corn, millet, safflower seed, and hulled sunflower seeds.

Of the five woodpeckers, two (yellow-bellied sapsucker and red-bellied woodpecker) are largely confined to eastern parts of the state, although the red-bellied woodpecker has been slowly working its way west along the Platte and other east-west river systems. All the woodpeckers other than sapsuckers will at times take corn, sunflower seeds, and other plant seeds, but suet and fat-rich "bird-puddings" are the favorite foods of all. Flickers are attracted to suet in winter and will sometimes take larger seeds such as corn. Red-bellied woodpeckers cache much of the food that they collect at feeders; the other species tend to consume it as they find it. During the 2011–12 Nebraska Christmas Counts, downy woodpeckers were seen in the greatest numbers, followed by northern flickers, red-bellied woodpeckers, hairy woodpeckers, and yellow-bellied sapsuckers.

The corvids (jays, crows, and magpies) are highly intelligent and highly observant birds. Jays are often the first to arrive and investigate whenever a fresh supply of food is put out, and crows have an uncanny ability to show up almost immediately after any poultry or other meat wastes are made available. Jays often appear in small groups of four or five birds, presumably family groups, and are able to keep most other birds away from the food, with the exception of large woodpeckers and crows. Crows and magpies also most often tend to arrive in pairs or up to four birds; magpies are especially prone to cache most of what they find. A blue jay may stuff twenty or more sunflower seeds into its gullet before flying off to cache them. During the 2011–12 Nebraska Christmas Counts, American crows were most often seen, followed by blue jays and magpies. The West Nile epidemic of 2002–03 had long-term disastrous effects on the corvid family. Magpie numbers still remain very low, and blue jays are only slowly recovering.

Among the most popular of all feeder birds are chickadees, titmice, and nuthatches; all are notably "perky" and will tolerate close-range observations during the short time it takes for one to arrive, pick up a single seed, and then fly off to hide it somewhere nearby. Sunflower seeds are the favorite food of all species, although suet is also highly favored by nuthatches. During the 2011–12 Nebraska Christmas Counts, the most frequently seen members of this group were black-capped chickadees, followed by white-breasted nuthatches, red-breasted nuthatches, tufted titmice, and pygmy nuthatches.

Other suet-loving and bird-pudding species include the kinglets, wrens, and brown creeper. Of the two kinglets, the golden-crowned is much more likely to overwinter in Nebraska than is the ruby-crowned, but the latter is more likely to show up at feeders, especially if suet-based or peanut-butter mixes (bird-puddings) are available. Kinglets are the smallest of Nebraska's wintering birds, weighing about six grams, or only twice the weight of our hummingbirds. During the 2011–12 Nebraska Christmas Counts, the most frequently seen birds of this group were golden-crowned kinglets, followed by brown creepers and Carolina wrens. A very few winter wrens, marsh wrens, and ruby-crowned kinglets were also reported.

Robins, bluebirds, and cedar waxwings are attracted to feeders with dried fruits and, in the case of the waxwing, red-cedar and mountain ash berries. All of these species are highly mobile during winter and often leave the state during severe winters. During the 2011–12 Nebraska Christmas Counts, the most frequently seen species of this group were American robins, followed by cedar waxwings, eastern bluebirds, and mountain bluebirds.

Nearly all of the seed-eating sparrow-like birds are attracted to feeders. However, the ground-foraging sparrows, such as American tree sparrows, towhees, and some grassland sparrows, are often reluctant to land on elevated platforms and are much more likely to scratch about on the ground below a feeder than fly up to it. Of the two Nebraska towhees, only the spotted is prone to overwinter, and only in southeastern Nebraska. Of the typical sparrows, the American tree sparrow is probably the most abundant in winter, but, like the Harris's sparrow, it is more likely to be found in rural locations than in cities. During the 2011–12 Nebraska Christmas Bird Counts, the most frequently seen birds of this group were American tree sparrows, followed by dark-eyed juncos, northern cardinals, Harris's sparrows, white-crowned sparrows, song sparrows, white-throated sparrows, and a few other rarely overwintering sparrows.

References

Dunn, E. H., and D. L. Tessaglia-Hymes. 1999. *Birds at Your Feeder: A Guide to Feeding Habits, Behavior, Distribution, and Abundance.* New York: Norton.

Johnsgard, P. A. 1998. A half-century of winter bird surveys at Lincoln and Scottsbluff, Nebraska. *Nebraska Bird Review* 66(3):74–84. http://digitalcommons.unl.edu/nebbirdrev/38/

Johnsgard, P. A. 2006. Recent changes in winter bird numbers at Lincoln, Nebraska. *Nebraska Bird Review* 74(1):16–22. http://digitalcommons.unl.edu/nebbirdrev/294/

Johnsgard, P. A. 2009. *Four Decades of Christmas Bird Counts in the Great Plains: Ornithological Evidence of a Changing Climate.* Range maps by T. G. Shane. 334 pp. http://digitalcommons.unl.edu/biosciornithology/46/

Johnsgard, P. A. 2013. Nebraska bird-feeder birds: What's in your backyard? *Prairie Fire,* February 2013, pp. 2, 5, 6. http://www.prairiefirenewspaper.com/2013/02/ nebraska-bird-feeder-birds-whats-in-your-backyard

4

The Grouse with the Pointed Tail

Nebraska is one of only two states (South Dakota is the other) that currently supports thriving populations of both sharp-tailed grouse and greater prairie-chickens, both of which are largely dependent on large areas of native grasslands for their survival. However, both species have undergone major changes in range and status during the past 150 years. Prior to the Civil War, the center of the greater prairie-chicken's distribution was in the tallgrass prairies of the Ohio and Mississippi River valleys but probably extended west to the southeastern corner of what became the state of Nebraska. In the heart of their historic range they probably supplemented their basic diets of native grass seeds with the increasingly available agricultural grain crops, such as corn and wheat.

As Nebraska and the Dakotas became more cultivated and reliant on small-grain agriculture, the greater prairie-chicken thrived on these new and reliable winter food sources. It spread its range westward with surprising speed, eventually reaching as far northwest as southern Alberta. This range expansion of the prairie-chicken lasted only a few decades, for soon after the start of the twentieth century the majority of the Midwest's tallgrass prairies had been converted to agriculture, leaving ever-fewer native prairies. This technological revolution in agriculture turned the tide of fortune against prairie-chickens, and they began to disappear from their acquired range almost as fast as they had acquired it. By midcentury the largest remaining continental populations of greater prairie-chickens were limited to Kansas, Nebraska, and the Dakotas.

On the other hand, the prairie race of the sharp-tailed grouse probably historically ranged over nearly all of what would become Nebraska and the Dakotas, and never became dependent on agricultural foods. It survived as well or better in the mixed-grass and Sandhills prairies to the west of the tallgrass region than it did benefiting from any contact with agricultural practices. Thus, the sharp-tailed grouse simply retreated before the plow, finding its most secure regional habitats in the Nebraska Sandhills.

This shifting of both species' ranges brought the sharp-tail and prairie-chickens into increasing contact, and by the 1920s hybrids had been reported from as far west as Nebraska, the Dakotas, Alberta, and Saskatchewan. During large-scale studies of Nebraska and South Dakota display grounds (leks) that were surveyed by state biologists during the 1950s and 1960s, 72 leks were observed to contain males of both species, and 26 of these grounds had hybrids present. Additionally, at least 15 hybrids were present among more than 1,200 prairie grouse trapped in Nebraska between 1950 and 1965. During a recent Nebraska Game and Parks Commission survey of about 200 leks, 4 percent were found to have males of both species present.

In an analysis I made several decades ago, I determined that mixed display grounds are most frequent where both species are fairly common but usually contain only one or two males of the less common species. The calculated incidence of mixed display grounds was far lower than would be expected by chance, but the presence of hybrids indicates that prairie-chickens and sharp-tailed grouse are not so distantly related as their courtship displays might suggest, and that at times their social interactions reach distinctly personal levels. Beyond the many genetic and evolutionary problems posed by the presence of these mixed-species leks and resulting hybrids, they offer fascinating opportunities for field studies and casual observations.

Sharp-tailed grouse are virtually the same size as greater prairie-chickens, averaging only a few ounces less in adult body mass, but their plumage patterns are quite different. Beyond their distinctive sharply pointed tails, sharp-tails have grayish brown upperparts and flanks that are flecked with white, so the birds become nearly invisible when crouched in a snowy, grass-poor landscape. In contrast, the vertically barred rich umber and buff feathers of prairie-chickens make them hard to detect in tall, dead-grass surroundings.

Although both species are similarly inconspicuous when trying to avoid detection, during courtship display they could hardly be more different. For example, the pointed tail of sharp-tails is held erect and conspicuously shaken during that species' unique "dancing" display. Prairie-chickens also erect their rather uniformly elongated and squared-off tails, but rather than shaking them, the feathers are widely and rather slowly spread during the "booming" display, and then are quickly snapped shut, producing a soft snapping sound.

Rapid foot-drumming sounds are produced by males of both species. In the sharp-tail, the stamping is much more prolonged and rapid (up to about twenty per second), whereas in the prairie-chicken stamping serves only as a short prelude to the male's much more obvious booming display. During booming, the male prairie-chicken's elongated and ornate neck feathers are erected, exposing two patches of orange skin on the sides of his neck. As these so-called "air sacs" are inflated by air pumped into the esophagus, a soft and resonant three-note phrase is uttered. This haunting call might easily be mistaken for a dove's, but it is much more hypnotic and can be heard over great distances. The resulting combination of visual and acoustic signals is perhaps the single most important attractant to female prairie-chickens ready to be mated, and probably attracts them from distances of up to a mile or more away.

In contrast, the male sharp-tail has a "cooing" display somewhat comparable to the prairie-chicken's booming, but the associated call is neither so loud nor so penetrating, and the bare violet-tinted rather than orange neck skin areas are smaller and not so conspicuously inflated. The cooing display is also relatively infrequent as compared with the prairie-chicken's frequent and conspicuous booming.

The visually most impressive part of the male sharp-tail's display repertoire is his prolonged and rapid foot stamping and march-like display, usually called "dancing." This remarkable display is performed with the male's head held low, his tail raised, and both wings

36

outstretched, so that he resembles a small toy airplane trying vainly to take off. The associated foot movements produce a pattern of erratic twists and turns, as if the airplane were being manned by a drunken pilot. The vigorous foot stamping also causes the erect tail feathers to rock rapidly from side to side, forcing their shafts to scrape noisily over one another. The males' combined foot-stamping and tail-scraping movements produce a low-pitched buzzing noise that is audible over surprisingly long distances and presumably attracts females in the same manner as does booming by prairie-chickens.

Another feature that sets the sharp-tail's dancing display apart from the prairie chicken's booming is the synchronicity of the participants. The dancing male sharp-tails all typically both start and stop their dancing abruptly and simultaneously. During the stationary phase of their dance, the birds stand perfectly still, as if their starts and stops were being precisely controlled by some unseen director. Perhaps these periodic silences allow the birds to hear any sounds made by an approaching threat.

There are other differences in the male behaviors of these two closely related species, as well as many important similarities. Basically, the arena-like composition of the participating males is exactly the same, such as the presence of a single dominant male, or "master cock," at each lek. This male is able to occupy and control, by threats and fighting, the most favorable lek location, and achieves the vast majority of the matings through both his social status and his heterosexual attraction.

These complex male mating behaviors probably serve two important biological roles. First, they allow each female to identify quickly the most genetically and physically fit available male as her best mating choice. Second, the marked differences between the two species in the males' posturing, vocalizations, and behaviors serve to exaggerate their dissimilarities and help prevent females from making mistakes during their hurried mating choices. Making a correct choice is important because the two species' genetic differences are too small to prevent the production of fully fertile hybrids. These visual and acoustic divergences in male behaviors thus serve as evolved "isolating mechanisms" that may play important roles in maintaining each species' genetic integrity.

Yet, in the glory of an April sunrise, and in the midst of a dozen or more gorgeous birds performing fantastic and archaic rituals with all the precision of a professional ballet company, it is easy to forget these aspects of theoretical biology and simply become immersed and entranced by the magic of the moment.

References

Johnsgard, P. A. 2010. The drums of April. *Prairie Fire*, April 2010, pp. 12–13. http://www.prairiefirenewspaper.com/2010/04/the-drums-of-april

Johnsgard, P. A. 2002. *Grassland Grouse and Their Conservation*. Washington, D.C.: Smithsonian Institution Press. 157 pp.

Johnsgard, P. A. 2013. The greater prairie-chicken: Spirit of the tallgrass prairie. *Prairie Fire*, April 2013, pp. 14–15. http://www.prairiefirenewspaper.com/2013/04/the-greater-prairie-chicken-spirit-of-the-tallgrass-prairie

Johnsgard, P. A. 2013. The grouse with the pointed tail. *Prairie Fire*, April 2013, pp. 16–18. http://www.prairiefirenewspaper.com/2013/04/the-grouse-with-the-pointed-tail

Paothong, N., and J. M. Vance. 2012. *Save the Last Dance: A Story of North American Grassland Grouse*. Columbia, MO: N. Paothong.

5

Grebes, Godwits, and Other Gifts
of Glaciers Past

Probably at some point about ten thousand to twenty thousand years ago, the vast Wisconsin phase of the glacier sheet that covered much of what is now the Dakotas and eastern Nebraska ground to a halt, and slowly began to retreat. The leading edges of the glacier stalled out near what is now the eastern edge of the Missouri River valley. As they did, shearing stresses in the ice resulted in large amounts of sediment that had been transported south by the glacier being shifted about. During melting, these sediments, including rocks and boulders as large as small cars, were deposited haphazardly. The resulting "dead-ice" moraines produced a region of small hills and intervening valleys extending from Alberta to northeastern Nebraska.

The valleys in this gently hilly "coteau" region (French for "little hill") quickly filled with glacial meltwaters and subsequent seasonal precipitation, producing the thousands of "prairie potholes" for which the region is known. These wetlands eventually developed into the shallow cattail- and rush-lined marshes that have since attracted countless water birds, the so-called "duck factory" region of the northern Great Plains.

Over time, the glacial meltwaters of the northern plains generated many large lakes, of which Manitoba's lakes Winnipeg and Winnipegosis are surviving remnants. Glacial Lake Agassiz also formed in what is now eastern North Dakota and western Minnesota. Most of its waters eventually drained southward into the Minnesota River valley, leaving only a small remnant Red River to develop and drain northward into Canada. Some very large rivers, such as the Missouri and Mississippi, as well as many smaller ones such as the Sheyenne,

also formed as the glacier retreated northward. The latter, inconspicuous river originates near the geographic center of North Dakota, and,
like a drunken cow, trudges erratically through the eastern half of
the state. Initially it passes slowly eastward through moraine-sculpted
landscapes south of Lakota in Nelson County, then turns southward,
eastward again, and finally northward, where it at last empties into
the Red River, north of Fargo.

In late glacial times, the Sheyenne drained into glacial Lake Agassiz, forming a broad, fertile delta in what is now northern Richland
County. The region where my mother's family farmed is adjacent to
the Sheyenne National Grassland, the only significant area of tallgrass
prairie remaining in North Dakota. There I first saw and learned to
identify native prairie plants and came to love such breeding birds as
marbled godwits and bobolinks. In prairie marshes west and south
of the table-flat and wheat-field covered Red River Valley, near my
teenage hometown of Wahpeton, I found a wetland paradise. I gradually learned to identify the common marshland birds and tried in-
effectually to photograph them. In the spring I joyfully waded these
marshes, as flocks of snow geese and Canadas passed by directly overhead, while individual great blue herons, great egrets, black-crowned
night-herons, and American bitterns sometimes erupted unexpectedly from the dense reed thickets.

Of all the marsh birds I encountered there, none was more en-
trancing than the western grebe. I saw it only rarely, as it was as beautiful and elusive as the Lady of the Lake, and the very essence of grace.
I called it the "swan grebe," for it has an impossibly long and gracefully
curved neck, a bicolored black-and-white head pattern, a rapier-like
yellow beak, and flaming red eyes. In the spring two adults could often be seen swimming side by side, performing synchronized preening and bowing displays to one another. Both would frequently utter soft calls that have been described as sounding like the tinkling of
silver bells. At times two or more of the birds would also madly rush
over the water for twenty to thirty yards, churning the water behind
them, and end this amazing display with simultaneous dives.

It wasn't until almost a half century later that I first held a live western grebe. On a spring visit to Nebraska's Crescent Lake National Wildlife Refuge I saw one beached on the shore of a large alkaline marsh. Grebes never voluntarily venture onto land, as their legs are positioned so far back that they are virtually helpless out of water. When I picked up the bird, I saw that one of its legs had been cleanly amputated, almost certainly by a snapping turtle. As a result, the grebe was doomed and likely to starve, or to be killed by another predator. Yet, in looking into its laser-red eyes I was unable to bring myself to mercifully end this marvelous creature's life. With tears in my eyes, I carefully placed it back where I had found it.

In 2014 I received an email from Deb Hanson, a resident of Grand Forks, North Dakota. She is an avid bird photographer and from her reading knew of my love for North Dakota and its water birds. She told me that northeastern North Dakota had been receiving record-breaking rainfall over the past twenty or so years, and the region's wetlands were overflowing. Her favorite birding area is about seventy miles west of Grand Forks in Nelson County, near the town of Lakota.

Although I couldn't arrange to get to North Dakota in 2014, in the spring of 2015 I asked her if water and bird conditions were still comparable. She answered in the affirmative, and noted that she had at times seen as many as 83 bird species during a single spring day, including eared, western, red-necked, and pied-billed grebes and almost uncountable numbers of shorebirds and waterfowl. I soon convinced a friend we should travel to North Dakota for a week of birding in late May. Driving north, we endured two days of cold rain and occasional ice pellets and high winds but took hope in the stoic opinion of local Dakotans that things could only improve. Over five inches of rain had fallen by our arrival.

At last we arrived at Lakota, a town of about eight hundred residents, and the only one with a motel within about twenty-five miles. We devised a twenty-six-mile rectangular survey route, with Lakota at its southeastern corner, extending north eight miles and east five miles. During three days of mostly car-window birding we saw more than 70 species, including 11 species of waterfowl and 22 species of shorebirds, gulls, and wading birds. On our last morning we did an hour-long, nonstop, nonbinocular twenty-five-miles-per-hour auto survey, counting both wetlands and bird "encounters" (each encounter consisted of one or more localized birds of a species).

In descending frequencies, our bird encounter totals were: eared grebe, American coot, western grebe, mallard, blue-winged teal, Canada goose, gadwall, lesser scaup, double-crested cormorant, Forster's tern, Franklin's gull, black-crowned night-heron, redhead, and (with one encounter each) pied-billed grebe, American white pelican, northern pintail, ruddy duck, American bittern, white-faced ibis, and black tern.

Clearly, North Dakota is a phenomenal region for watching water and marsh birds. The four or five days of freezing weather that occurred before we arrived had placed swallows and aerial insect-eaters such as kingbirds into near-starving conditions. We saw many barn swallows, western kingbirds, and Swainson's thrushes, as well as upland sandpipers, willets, and marbled godwits, foraging on the county roads for dead or moribund insects. As the weather improved, flying swallows and black terns became more evident, as did insects.

We commonly observed courtship and territorial behavior among coots, two grebes, and several ducks, including ruddy ducks. The last-named species perhaps has the most remarkable display of all North American ducks. Males have an inflatable tracheal air sac, which produces a soft sound when he slaps his bill on his chest, causing a semicircle of bubbles to appear as air is forced out of his breast feathers.

An equally remarkable behavior is present in the American bittern, and we were fortunate enough to witness this rarely seen activity. While uttering his strange low-pitched "thunder-pump" call, seemingly achieved by inflating his esophagus rather than his trachea. The male periodically would make his otherwise fully camouflaged presence known by exposing a pair of conspicuous fan-shaped clusters of immaculate white plumes emerging from just in front of its folded wings. On both of the occasions when I have observed such plume exhibition, a female was standing within about thirty to forty yards of the male. When I observed it previously this display activity eventually led to a copulation. We watched for twenty minutes, when the birds flew farther into the marsh.

Among our observed wetlands, more than 100 were temporary run-off depressions, 36 were small rush- and cattail-filled wetlands with no visible water, 45 were wetlands with up to 100 yards of open water, and 41 had areas of open water greater than 100 yards across. A few wetlands covered almost an entire square-mile section, and one marsh—"McHugh Slough"—extended for more than four miles. At least four of the four-way road intersections we crossed had extensive marsh-like wetlands in all directions. Our auto route also passed near seven deserted (mostly flooded) farmsteads.

By comparison, a much larger wetland survey over the entire glaciated region of eastern South Dakota revealed more than 520,000 temporary wetlands, over 33,000 seasonal wetlands, almost 24,000 semi-permanent wetlands, and over 600 permanent wetlands, collectively occupying nearly 500 square miles, or less than 1 percent of the land surface. About 100 species each of associated birds and fish, 25 mammals, 17 amphibians, and 10 reptiles use these wetlands (Johnson et al., 1997). No other Great Plains habitat would come remotely close to supporting such species diversity per unit area.

A week is far too short a time to visit all the magnificent wetlands of North Dakota. With twenty-four national wildlife refuges and wetland management districts, North Dakota leads the nation in the total number of nationally preserved wetlands. However, the state still lacks a modern book-length documentation of its total bird fauna. Some of the refuges we visited showed signs of neglect and reduced staffing resulting from federal budget-cutting. Neither we nor the hundreds of wildlife species depending on wetland habitats can afford such poor shepherding of our country's marvelous natural resources.

References

Johnsgard, P. A. 1980. Copulatory behavior in the American bittern. *Auk* 97:868–869.

Johnsgard, P. A. 2012a. *Nebraska's Wetlands: Their Wildlife and Ecology.* Water Survey Paper No. 78. Lincoln: Conservation and Survey Division, IANR, University of Nebraska–Lincoln. 202 pp.

Johnsgard, P. A. 2012b. *Wetland Birds of the Central Plains: South Dakota, Nebraska, and Kansas.* Lincoln: Zea Books and University of Nebraska–Lincoln DigitalCommons http://digitalcommons.unl.edu/zeabook/8/. 275 pp. Print edition available from http://www.lulu.com/shop/paul-johnsgard/.

Johnson, R. R., K. F. Higgins, M. L. Kjellsen, and C. R. Elliott. 1997. *Eastern South Dakota Wetlands.* Brookings: South Dakota State University. 28 pp.

6

Climate Change and Altered Bird Migrations in the Great Plains

When I was a youngster in North Dakota during the 1940s and 1950s, the seasons were very obvious and clear-cut to me. For example, I knew that the peak of fall foliage color would occur early in September. Most small birds would be gone by the end of that month, and the major waterfowl migration of ducks and geese would occur in October. By the first of November fall was usually over, and winter snowstorms could strike at any time. Then it would be an infinitely long wait until the spring thaw, and I could not expect to see even early waterfowl migrants, such as snow geese, returning to the prairie marshes of southeastern North Dakota until early April. Sadly, they would stay only a few short weeks before pushing north as rapidly as the melting ice would allow.

After moving to Nebraska in the early 1960s, my seasonal biological calendar for fall and spring had to be reset by several weeks. The fall foliage peak was likely not to occur until about the end of September. The arctic-breeding snow geese would begin appearing in early October, reaching a peak at about the end of that month, or sometimes in early November. That calendar was so reliable that, when I was involved in an NETV documentary in the late 1980s, I could advise the producer several months in advance that, to catch the main snow goose migration at Squaw Creek National Wildlife Refuge in northwestern Missouri, we would need to reserve an expensive telephoto lens for their movie camera for the third week in October.

During the decades extending from the 1960s through the start of the twenty-first century, many ecological changes occurred in the northern hemisphere. These were reflected in altered bird migration

45

patterns throughout the central Great Plains, especially as to their timing, magnitude, and destinations. During the late 1960s, snow geese gradually began to arrive in Nebraska ever later in the fall, and to build up in even greater numbers. By the late 1970s, vast numbers of snow geese would stage briefly at DeSoto National Wildlife Refuge near Blair, Nebraska, and a few weeks later fly south about one hundred miles to the Squaw Creek refuge to remain until freeze-up.

Changes in goose numbers were dramatic. When I first visited Squaw Creek in the early 1960s, snow goose numbers typically peaked there at about 150,000 birds. By 1978 the snow geese at Squaw Creek peaked at 280,000. These numbers reached 350,000 by 1982 and had attained a record high of 600,000 by 1986. Since then the refuge's peak snow goose numbers have at times reached a million birds.

These increasing goose numbers have been mainly attributed to the increased grain crops available locally to the geese and to the safety from waterfowl hunters provided by a series of strategically placed national wildlife refuges located between North Dakota and the Gulf Coast. Warmer and longer breeding seasons in the arctic have no doubt also benefited snow goose populations across North America. Snow geese have also remained around Squaw Creek progressively later in the fall during the past six decades. Increasing numbers stay there well after freeze-up by moving to nearby deeper and more ice-free waters such as Big Lake, and they also commonly overwinter in the nearby Missouri River valley.

To illustrate changes in migration timing, in 1966 and 1967 snow geese arrived at Squaw Creek during the second and third weeks of September, and their numbers peaked at an average of 165,000 during the last week of October and first week of November. They had nearly all departed by the end of December. By comparison, between 2008 and 2012 maximum numbers ranged from 390,000 to 1,425,000 birds, typically peaking in late November or early December. In 2013 they didn't arrive until the first week of November. In the past few years snow geese have remained in the general vicinity of Squaw Creek all winter, even though outside the refuge's boundaries they have been subjected to intense hunting pressures during an extended hunting season that lasts at least through January.

A similar delayed migration was happening to Canada geese and cackling geese along the Platte River in central Nebraska during these same decades, with their numbers gradually increasing to about 100,000 birds overwintering in the Platte valley by the early 2000s. Smaller numbers of snow geese, Ross's geese, and greater white-fronted geese likewise now sometimes overwinter in the state. Sandhill cranes have overwintered in the central Platte valley in substantial numbers since 2011.

By the early 2000s it was clear to biologists, as had been concluded much earlier by climatologists, that the world is not now as it had been and that a long-term climatic warming trend had arrived. An extended nine-year drought and unusually warm summer temperatures brought the news home to Nebraska in 2002. The drought lasted nearly a decade and was followed by a return visit in 2013. While a few Nebraska politicians have professed that the warming trend was only an unavoidable cyclical event rather than an indicator of a long-term climate change resulting largely from human influences, the facts speak to the contrary.

Using the National Audubon Society's annual Christmas count data obtained from the mid-1960s onward, evidence of a long-term trend toward milder winters is apparent in the Great Plains. In Kansas, Nebraska, and even into the Dakotas more water-dependent bird species such as waterfowl and gulls are now regularly present at least until the end of December.

In counts from Lincoln, Nebraska, the greatest increases in late-December birds over the past half-century have occurred among the Canada goose, mallard, and ring-billed gull. Three species of ducks and two species of sandpipers have recently appeared on the Lincoln counts for the first time, and among terrestrial species there have been great increases in the numbers of American robins and red-winged blackbirds.

Other species that usually winter farther south and have increased to a lesser degree are the eastern bluebird, golden-crowned kinglet, and yellow-rumped warbler; both the bluebird and kinglet now regularly overwinter locally.

In contrast, some species have gradually declined in the Christmas counts for Lincoln and now tend to concentrate farther to the north and west in Nebraska, or in the Dakotas. These include various boreal forest and arctic-breeding species such as the snow bunting, Lapland longspur, common redpoll, and evening grosbeak.

In 2008 I decided to try to test the broad-scale influence of this warming trend by analyzing the late-December distributions of migratory birds throughout the Great Plains, using data from the National Audubon Society's annual Christmas Bird Count. With the help of my ornithology students one recent summer, we determined the mean state-by-state abundances of more than 200 bird species in late December, from North Dakota south through the Texas panhandle. This analysis covered the period 1968–69 to 2007–8 by ten-year intervals (Johnsgard, 2009).

Determining the five most common species in each of the Great Plains states over each ten-year interval provides a useful overview of major regional population shifts among late fall and early winter birds. In North Dakota the most common bird on Christmas counts for the decade 1968–77 was the house sparrow; the Canada goose was not among the top five most common species. However, by the decade 1998–2007 the Canada goose was the most common species, followed by the house sparrow; the mallard had by then climbed to fourth place.

In South Dakota the most common bird on Christmas counts for the decade 1968–77 was the mallard; the house sparrow was second, and the Canada goose was fifth. However, by the decade 1998–2007 the mallard was the most common species, followed by the Canada goose. The house sparrow had by then fallen to fifth place.

In Nebraska the most common bird on Christmas counts for the decade 1968–77 was the mallard; the house sparrow was third, and the Canada goose was fifth. During the decade 1998–2007, the mallard was still the most common species, followed by the Canada goose; the house sparrow was not then in the top five.

In Kansas and in Oklahoma the most common species reported for the decade 1968–77 was the red-winged blackbird; it was still in first place for the decade 1998–2007 in both states. In Kansas the greater white-fronted goose had risen to fourth place by the decade 1998–2007, while in Oklahoma the snow goose had reached fifth place.

These relatively few examples clearly point out some of the strong biological effects of very small annual changes in temperature. Over the nearly eleven decades between 1895 and 2008, the average January temperature increased 0.44 degree Fahrenheit per decade in North Dakota (collectively, 4.7 degrees), 0.19 degree in South Dakota, 0.11 degree in Nebraska, 0.10 degree in Kansas, and 0.04 degree in Oklahoma (collectively 1.9 degrees), showing that regional warming is proceeding most rapidly at northern latitudes. It is likely that life in the Great Plains is destined only to get warmer. Even armadillos, not generally thought to be smarter than our dullest state senators, have gotten the message and increasing numbers have been trudging north into Nebraska.

References

Johnsgard, P. A. 1998. A half-century of winter bird surveys at Lincoln and Scottsbluff, Nebraska. *Nebraska Bird Review* 66:74–84. http://digitalcommons.unl.edu/nebbirdrev/38/

Johnsgard, P. A. 2009. *Four Decades of Christmas Bird Counts in the Great Plains: Ornithological Evidence of a Changing Climate.* Distribution maps by T. G. Shane. http://digitalcommons.unl.edu/biosciornithology/46/.

Johnsgard, P. A. 2010. Snow geese on the Great Plains. *Prairie Fire*, February 2010, pp. 12–15. http://www.prairiefirenewspaper.com/2010/02/snow-geese-on-the-great-plains

Johnsgard, P. A. 2015. Climate change and its biological effects in the Great Plains. *Prairie Fire*, April 2015, pp. 6–8. http://www.prairiefirenewspaper.com/2015/04/climate-change-and-its-biological-effects-in-the-great-plains

Red-necked grebe

PART II

Sacred Places and Why They Matter

Whooping crane

7

Aransas National Wildlife Refuge:
The Whooping Crane's
Critical Winter Retreat

Perhaps no North American species of bird has come closer to extinction and yet managed to survive into the twenty-first century than has the whooping crane. The ratification and activation of the Migratory Bird Treaty Act of 1918 had brought the whooping cranes of Canada and the United States into complete protection, but by then probably no more than about sixty of these birds were still surviving. At least twenty-five more were killed during the next four years. By then it was apparent that most of the surviving birds were wintering in coastal Texas and migrating north to unknown breeding grounds somewhere in Canada. It was not until 1955 that the species' breeding grounds were discovered in an already-protected area on the border of Alberta and the Northwest Territories—Wood Buffalo National Park.

In Texas, a second tiny group of whooping cranes that had wintered on the vast King Ranch of southern Texas disappeared by 1937, leaving the last known wintering population of about a few dozen birds on the Blackjack Peninsula of coastal Texas north of Corpus Christi, between San Antonio and Aransas Bays. A small residential flock also then still survived in the prairies and coastal marshes of Louisiana, where a dozen or so birds had been found around White Lake during the construction of the Intracoastal Waterway in 1929.

Ironically, Myron Swenk, Nebraska's premier (and only) ornithologist of the 1930s, was responsible for the sadly mistaken belief that there were still perhaps three hundred whooping cranes still in existence during the 1930s. This assumption was based on unverified reports by volunteer birds watchers tallying spring migrants. These reports were subsequently published in the state's ornithological journal, *The Nebraska Bird Review*, and were accepted without question by the professional ornithologists of the American Ornithologists' Union, which thus failed to understand the gravity of the species' actual precarious status.

In another turn of irony, the Great Depression of the 1930s had the beneficial effect of stimulating the federal government to employ thousands of out-of-work people in the Civilian Conservation Corps. This workforce undertook innumerable conservation-oriented activities, such as constructing more than 800 parks nationwide, planting millions of trees, and developing roads and facilities for sites that were or were to become national parks and national wildlife refuges.

One of the many locations studied by the U.S. Department of the Interior and recommended for inclusion in the rapidly expanding system of national wildlife refuges during the 1930s was the Blackjack Peninsula. This area was the only known winter home of the entire remnant migratory whooping crane flock, and it was known for wintering a great variety of shorebirds and waterfowl. It also supported a resident population of the already rare Attwater's prairie-chicken, a race of the greater prairie-chicken endemic to the coastal prairies of Texas that by 1937 had already lost 93 percent of its original habitat, and whose population had been reduced from nearly a million birds to less than nine thousand.

In December of 1937, President Franklin D. Roosevelt signed an executive order creating the Aransas Migratory Waterfowl Refuge (later renamed the Aransas National Wildlife Refuge), purchasing land that encompassed much of Blackjack Peninsula, totaling more than 47,000 acres. The area's bargain-basement purchase (at about ten dollars per acre) unfortunately excluded control of grazing rights and mineral rights, both of which would later cause serious problems in refuge management. Additionally, shooting rights by a hunting club extended to the refuge's boundaries, threatening the safety of any cranes straying beyond the refuge. To make matters worse, in 1940 the U.S. Army Corps of Engineers began to dredge a channel for the expanding Gulf Intracoastal Waterway, cutting a three-hundred-foot-wide ditch and associated right-of-way through a previously isolated part of the refuge.

During the area's initial fall and winter of 1938–39, the refuge manager counted 14 whooping cranes, including two juveniles, causing him to estimate that a total of no more than 18 birds might be present, assuming that as many as 2 birds might have been overlooked. In the following fall five pairs returned with young, two of the pairs tending twins, and 5 other adults were also present, for a total of 22 birds.

In 1940 oil drilling began just outside the refuge's limits, and the Army Air Corps took over nearby Matagorda Island for military use. Along with nearby San José Island, this 56,000-acre barrier island was an important foraging area for the cranes and had been recommended for inclusion in the refuge, but the federal budget hadn't permitted its purchase.

During the fall of 1941, only 14 adult whooping cranes and 2 young returned to Aransas, a total that marks a historic population low point for the species, although 6 additional birds were then still surviving in Louisiana. The Louisiana flock was extirpated by 1950–51, as a probable result of coastal storms. By that time the Wood Buffalo–Aransas flock had increased by 20 birds, reaching a grand total of 34, but this total represented an average population gain of only 2 birds annually.

By the end of the next decade (1959–60), the Wood Buffalo–Aransas flock still hovered precariously at only 33 birds, but by the fall of 1969–70 it had gained another 23 birds, totaling 56. By 1979–80 the total was 76, and by 1989–90 the flock had experienced a burst of breeding success and had reached 146. At the turn of the twenty-first century, the autumn refuge total was 188 birds.

During the past century the Aransas refuge had more than its share of disappointments. Oil drilling, illegal shooting, and other disturbances along the Intracoastal Waterway became serious problems during the 1940s, and they still persist. During World War II, the

56,000-acre Matagorda Island was used as a practice bombing range by the Air Force, causing an unknown amount of disturbance and damage to the cranes. It was not until 1955, a year after the crane's nesting grounds in Wood Buffalo National Park were finally discovered, that the Air Force agreed not to undertake nighttime bombing practice on Matagorda Island, which would have caused a major wildlife disturbance. In 1973 the Aransas National Wildlife Refuge finally acquired management jurisdiction over much of Matagorda Island. In 1995 the entire island was named Matagorda Island Wildlife Management Area, to be managed jointly by the state and federal government for conserving rare and endangered birds and supporting migratory bird management.

Other chronic problems have long existed at Aransas. By 1970 heavy grazing by 2,500 to 4,000 cattle on the refuge had an impact on grassland-dependent birds such as the Attwater's prairie-chicken, and it eventually was extirpated from the area. Since then, grazing has been terminated, and the prairie conditions have improved, although invasive growth by shinnery oak is a significant problem. Periodic hurricanes have also ravaged the area. In August 1965 a major hurricane passing up the Texas coast slammed into Matagorda Island, illuminating the region's vulnerability to such storms. Luckily these increasingly frequent late-summer storms have so far occurred before the cranes are present on the refuge. Another impending ecological problem is the invasion of black mangroves into the region, which is likely to impact foraging opportunities for whooping cranes and other marshland foraging birds.

Disaster struck the Wood Buffalo–Aransas flock in the fall of 2008, with the onset of a prolonged drought in Texas. The major source of fresh water to Aransas National Wildlife Refuge is the Guadalupe River, which maintains the salinity of the coastal wetlands and allows for the survival of blue crabs, the whooping crane's major winter food. Increased drought-related diversions of this river water by Texas water authorities (the Texas Commission on Environmental Quality) resulted in an increased salinity of water around the Aransas refuge. These salinity changes decimated the local population of blue crabs and led to the death of at least 23 whooping cranes during the winter of 2008–09, reducing the crane population to 263 by the spring of 2009. A lawsuit filed in U.S. District Court in 2010 resulted in a finding three years later to the effect that such diversions violated the Endangered Species Act, and it initiated the development of a Habitat Conservation Plan for Whooping Cranes. This plan should reduce the likelihood of a repeat of the 2008–09 disaster, although the court's decision was later overturned when the 5th Circuit Court of Appeals ruled against the finding.

During 2011 the Wood Buffalo–Aransas flock built a record high of 75 nests and fledged about 37 young. In spite of that impressive nesting success, the winter 2011–12 population census at Aransas resulted in a total of only 254 birds within the primary survey area, although others were known to winter outside the survey's geographic limits. The Fish and Wildlife Service acknowledged that, because of sampling constraints associated with a less comprehensive winter survey protocol, the flock's size then could statistically have been anywhere from 199 to 325 birds. Such confidence limits are far greater than any historical annual population increase or decrease of the Wood Buffalo–Aransas flock, making it impossible to estimate the population trajectory of this vitally important population.

In 2012 a total of 31 families were counted at Wood Buffalo National Park, including two sets of twins, for a total of 33 chicks. No specific numbers have been released from the winter 2012–13 surveys of adults and juveniles at Aransas, other than the comment that it was generally believed that there probably were more than 250 birds in the wild flock. During the summer of 2013, 28 whooping crane chicks resulting from 74 nests were counted during a July survey. The winter surveys of 2014–15 at Aransas indicated that an estimated 304 cranes were present.

Since the establishment of Aransas National Wildlife Refuge, many other major conservation efforts have been undertaken toward preserving and restoring whooping cranes, and to produce a second flock independent of the Wood Buffalo–Aransas population. These have included an unsuccessful effort to hatch and raise whooping cranes using wild sandhill cranes as foster parents in Idaho, and a similarly unsuccessful effort to establish a resident whooping crane flock in the Kissimmee Prairie of Florida. In 2011, 10 hand-reared whooping cranes were introduced into the White Lake region of southwestern Louisiana, the start of a multi-year effort to reestablish a resident flock in that state. By the beginning of 2014 that flock had been increased to about 35 birds, but in February vandals shot and killed the female of a subadult pair that were building a practice nest, and seriously wounded the male, which later died.

The most innovative attempt is an audacious experiment—"Operation Migration"—involving the rearing of whooping cranes in Wisconsin and training them with the guidance of ultralight aircraft to migrate to Florida, in a heroic effort to establish an independent migratory flock in eastern North America. The success of this effort will ultimately depend on the abilities of these birds to successfully breed and rear young under wild conditions, including often lethal threats to the young from blood-draining bites by black flies. So far, the results of these efforts are still uncertain but promising.

Given the recent warming and drying climate trend in the Great Plains, and consequent increased losses of wetlands, the future of the Wood Buffalo–Aransas flock of whooping cranes is still by no means secure. However, without the establishment of Aransas National Wildlife Refuge at a critical time, the species would almost certainly have joined the passenger pigeon, Carolina parakeet, and Eskimo curlew on the dismal list of twentieth-century North American bird extinctions.

References

Gil-Weir, K., and Johnsgard, P. A. 2010. The whooping cranes: Survivors against all odds. *Prairie Fire*, September 2010, pp. 12, 13, 16, 22. http://www.prairiefirenewspaper.com/2010/09/the-whooping-cranes-survivors-against-all-odds

Hughes, J. M. 2008. *Cranes: A Natural History of a Bird in Crisis.* Buffalo, NY: FireflyBooks.

Johnsgard, P. A. 1991. *Crane Music: A Natural History of American Cranes.* Washington, D.C.: Smithsonian Institution Press.

Johnsgard, P. A. 2011. *Sandhill and Whooping Cranes: Ancient Voices over America's Wetlands.* Lincoln: University of Nebraska Press. 155 pp.

Johnsgard, P. A. 2014. Aransas National Wildlife Refuge: The whooping crane's vulnerable winter retreat. *Prairie Fire*, May 2014, pp. 12–13. http://www.prairiefirenewspaper.com/2014/05/aransas-national-wildlife-refuge-the-whooping-cranes-vulnerable-winter-retreat

Johnsgard, P. A. 2015. *A Chorus of Cranes: The Cranes of North America and the World.* (Photographs by Thomas D. Mangelsen.) Boulder: University Press of Colorado.

8

Secrets of the Very Long Dead:
Ashfall Fossil Beds State Historical Park

One day in the summer of 1971, the University of Nebraska's pale-ontologist Mike Voorhies and his wife, Jane, were walking along the streambed of a tributary of Verdigre Creek in Antelope County, gathering data for a planned geological map. Mike knew the area well, having grown up in the small town of Orchard, only eight miles away. Walking along the streambed ravine, he noticed an exposed layer of ash about a foot in thickness partway up the face of a steep slope.

(As a geological aside, this pale grayish ash layer is part of the widespread evidence of a volcanic explosion that occurred nearly 12 million years ago, during late Miocene times. The ash originated in what is now southwestern Idaho, where a gigantic hotspot of magma once erupted. Because the North American tectonic plate has drifted slowly to the west over the past 12 million years, the hotspot that produced the ash-layer eruption is currently located under Yellowstone National Park, where it is responsible for all of that region's thermal features and earthquake-prone landscape.)

As Mike walked along the ravine, he noticed a small fossilized jaw and teeth. After some careful excavation, the entire skull of a baby rhinoceros about a foot in length slowly emerged. Further excavation exposed some of the neck vertebrae, leading him to believe the entire skeleton might be present. Returning the next day, the baby rhino's entire skeleton emerged, as did three more, including one of an adult rhinoceros.

In spite of his excitement, time and equipment didn't then permit additional digging, but Mike recognized this site as the find of a lifetime. Under his direction in 1977 a museum crew began to remove the layer of sandstone above the volcanic deposits. From an exposed area of about two hundred square feet, the group collected several more rhino skeletons. With the support of a National Geographic grant, Mike brought a group of eight students back in 1978, and they began large-scale excavations over an area of about six thousand square feet.

By 1979 some two hundred skeletons of various mammals had been exposed from the volcanic matrix, in one part of which twelve rhino skeletons were clustered into an area not much bigger than the size of an average living room. The site had once been a watering hole that had gradually filled with ash. Lung failure, caused by inhaling the volcanic dust, eventually killed all the unlucky animals that had huddled together in it.

Besides the rhinos—which were robust, short-legged animals belonging to a genus (*Teleoceros*) known as the barrel-bodied rhinoceros—there were also five genera of horses, three of camels, and two members of the dog family. There was also a small saber-toothed deer that closely resembles the modern musk deer (*Mochus*) of Asia, whose distinctive protruding canine teeth are used by males for fighting. There were also smaller mammals, turtles, and a few birds. The smallest animals evidently died soonest, as their remains are largely situated at the lower level of the volcanic layer, with the middle-sized and larger animals being sequentially located above.

Most of the fossils found so far are of species that had previously been discovered, but what came to be known as the Ashfall Fossil Beds site is unique in the number and completeness of specimens, and the extremely high details of bone preservation. The tiny particles of volcanic dust served as a perfect casting material, preserving tiny body parts, such as the tiny middle ear bones of larger mammals and the windpipes of cranes. Other remarkable finds include feather impressions, an unborn rhino calf inside the skeleton of its mother, a bird skeleton with small pebbles that had once served for grinding food in its gizzard, and fossil grass seeds from the throat of a rhino. More than fifty species of plants and animals have been identified from the site.

No doubt the prize finds have been the numerous intact skeletons of rhinos, most of which lay crouched with their legs tucked under them, or lying on their sides. More than a dozen were found tending young as they died. The clustered grouping suggests that this rhinoceros was much more social than are the present-day species of rhinos, which tend to be solitary animals. Evidently, like elephants, these rhinos formed herds of adult females and calves, accompanied by single adult males. Of about one hundred skeletons, only seven were adult males, with adult females outnumbering them by a ratio of more than six to one. The staggered ages of the young indicates that they were born seasonally rather than throughout the year.

Some of the more notable finds, at least for bird lovers, were the skeletons of an extinct crane species that, at least in terms of its skeletal features, is nearly identical to the modern African crowned cranes. The two living species of crowned cranes are believed to be the most structurally generalized ("primitive") of all fifteen living cranes, with some unique features such as long hind toes that allow them to perch in trees. In contrast to the more advanced cranes, the windpipes of crowned cranes extend directly from the gullet to the lungs rather than forming a loop that penetrates the keel of the breastbone. This loop greatly extends the length of the windpipe, enhancing the birds' vocal resonating abilities and probably increasing the volume of their calls. The discovery of crowned cranes at Ashfall also proves that primitive cranes once ranged to North America, where now only the sandhill crane and whooping crane exist.

Several other species of fossil birds have also been found at Ashfall, including a hawk (*Apatosagittarius*) with convergent similarities to the modern African secretary bird. Another major recent discovery is a primitive vulture-like hawk, *Anchigyps voorhiesi*, which seems to connect anatomically the typical hawks and eagles with the Old World vultures, and which was named in honor of Mike Voorhies.

In common with these fossil birds, modern rhinos, camels, and wild horses now occur only in the Old World. This pattern shows how the distributions of many mammals and birds have shifted over the past 12 million years, and how evolution has molded them during the intervening timespan. For example, three of the five species that were found at Ashfall had feet with three well-developed toes that were probably useful for walking in soft terrain or in dodging predators. One species (*Protohippus*) also had three toes, but two of them were reduced in size and perhaps of no functional value. Another species, the large, single-toed *Pliohippus*, closely approached the modern horse, having broad hooves that are best adapted to running fast over hard surfaces but probably had limited cornering abilities.

In contrast, the toes of camels have evolved to allow walking over relatively soft substrates. Modern camel feet have two toes and undivided soles, helping to maximize each foot's surface area and spread their substantial body weight. Other than the rhinos and horses, camels were the most common large mammals found at Ashfall, with several dozen uncovered. Most of them are of a type called *Procamelus* that, as the name implies, is believed to have been ancestral to the true Old World camels.

Although initially researchers had to excavate the site in the open air, in 2009 a 17,500-square-foot building, the Hubbard Rhino Barn, replaced a much smaller earlier structure. Within the building, a walkway allows visitors a close view of the excavated skeletons, and of scientists continuing the excavation work.

Along the walls a large series of paintings are displayed, showing remarkably lifelike reconstructions of many examples of the area's rich fossil legacy. They are part of a larger series of about fifty paintings done by Mark Marcuson, depicting some of Ashfall's most iconic fossil animals. Mark also painted the large mural in the visitor center, showing the doomed rhinos in their watering hole. A group of *Pliohippus* horses is leaving the watering hole, while other horses, camels, and cranes can all be seen nearby, along with some distant elephants. Although so far none has been found at Ashfall, elephants have been found in nearby Niobrara excavations.

The Ashfall Fossil Beds was made a state park in 1991 and named a National Natural Landmark in 2006. The park is located two miles east and six miles north of Royal, in northern Antelope County. Its visitor center includes a preparation laboratory, interpretive displays, and small gift shop with a good selection of books. Surrounding the excavation is a large area of restored mixed-grass prairie, where wildflowers and typical grassland birds such as western meadowlarks, dickcissels, and upland sandpipers can usually be seen.

The 360-acre park is open Monday through Saturday, 9 a.m. to 5 p.m., Memorial Day to Labor Day, with limited hours in May, September, and October. Paleontologists from the University of Nebraska State Museum and interpretive staff are present; the Nebraska Game and Parks Commission oversees the park and its maintenance. Admission is $5 for adults and $3 for children over five years old. Holders of current Nebraska state park permits are admitted free; daily or annual park permits are on sale at the site. Information can be obtained at 402-893-2000 or at http://ashfall.unl.edu/.

References

Bouc, K. (coordinator). 1994. The Cellars of Time: Paleontology and Archeology in Nebraska. *Nebraska History* 75(1):1–162.

Garbino, M. 2012. Worldtour: Ashfall Fossil Beds, Nebraska. *Smithsonian Magazine* 42(9):48–49.

Johnsgard, P. A. 2014. Secrets of the very long dead: Ashfall Fossil Beds State Historical Park. *Prairie Fire*, October 2014, pp. 1, 3, 4. http://www.prairiefirenewspaper.com/2014/10/secrets-of-the-very-long-dead-ashfall-fossil-beds-state-historical-park

Voorhies, M. R., A. Griffiths, and J. H. Matternes. 1981. Ancient ashfall creates a Pompeii of prehistoric animals, dwarfing the St. Helens eruption. *National Geographic Magazine* 159(1):66–75.

9

Squaw Creek National Wildlife Refuge: Gem of the Missouri Valley

During July 1804, Lewis and Clark traversed up the middle Missouri River valley, through a region that is now part of northwestern Missouri. On July 12, near the mouth of the Big Nemaha River, they observed some "artificial mounds," representing the locations of ancient Native American graves. There they also saw many Canada geese families along the river. Now, 200 years later, the Big Nemaha River is a tiny, muddy remnant of its once eighty-yard width, and all traces of the burial mounds are gone. A small town, Mound City, has developed near here along the eastern edge of the valley, and a stream with the anachronistic name of Squaw Creek provides critical water for Squaw Creek National Wildlife Refuge (NWR). And, from late fall through early spring, upwards of a million or more birds stop at this refuge while on their migration north and south, arriving from breeding grounds as far north as Canada's high arctic tundra and heading toward wintering grounds as far south as southern South America.

Squaw Creek NWR is located at the eastern edge of the Missouri River valley, about two miles south of Mound City, Missouri, reached via exit 79 off I-29. It was established in the 1930s, after early twentieth-century efforts to farm the frequently flooded bottomlands failed, and the land reverted to the federal government. By using a series of low dikes and water-control structures, nearly half of the refuge's approximate 7,400 acres is maintained as shallow marshland, with the rest being deciduous woodlands, pastures, and croplands.

The refuge is flanked to the east by steep, forested loess hills that are more than 150 feet high. They were formed by deep deposits of silt blown in from the west and deposited along the river valley during late Pleistocene times. The nearby Missouri River is no longer the mile-wide shallow and snag-strewn river known intimately by Lewis and Clark. Since the 1940s, it has been diverted, diked, dredged, and dammed, the results of seventy years of spectacularly unsuccessful efforts by the U.S. Army Corps of Engineers to prevent flooding and to keep the channel deep enough to support today's nearly nonexistent barge traffic. Now it is a biologically degraded waterway, confined regionally to a six-hundred-foot-wide channel and a consequent rapid stream flow that is prone to periodically catastrophic floods.

In this region, the Missouri valley's north-south orientation, its historically rich bottomland farms, and its extensive marshes provide a powerful magnet for migrating waterfowl, shorebirds, and other water-dependent migrants. The adjacent wooded hillsides provide natural migratory guidelines for hawks, vultures, and eagles using updraft winds on which to effortlessly soar and glide during migration, and tree-dependent songbirds also use these forested hillsides as migratory corridors and brief stopover sites.

Shortly after arriving in Nebraska in 1961 I sought out this famous refuge and thereafter have never missed a migration season without visiting it at least once. Even as early as the 1960s, the refuge supported fall populations of several hundred thousand snow geese, out of a continental population of then perhaps two million birds, as well as large numbers of other waterfowl. During subsequent decades, the national snow goose population has progressively increased, and Squaw Creek's migrant population has continued to thrive. From the years 2008 through 2011, for example, the maximum yearly numbers of snow geese at the refuge have ranged from about 390,000 to 1,425,000 birds. Peak numbers depend on the onset of winter weather, but during normal years, the largest numbers are likely to be seen in late November or early December, and again in early March. Some 20 percent to 25 percent of the Missouri valley geese are mostly brown-plumaged blue geese, a color variation that is the result of a genetic mutation of unknown survival significance.

There are also many variably intermediate plumages produced by the mating of snow and blue plumage types, confounding easy field identification.

In recent years some Ross's geese, miniature relatives of the snow goose that are a little larger than mallards, have also been increasing. These tiny geese are often overlooked among the much larger snow geese, but an all-time maximum of 440 were observed in 1987. A few hybrids between snow geese and Ross's geese have also been reported, further complicating field identification.

Because of commercial and private waterfowl hunting around the refuge's perimeter, large numbers of snow geese are shot each fall. Some of the birds that are only wounded manage to make their way back to the refuge limits, gradually resulting in a small flock of flightless or nearly flightless birds. This supply of variably incapacitated geese produces a rich bounty of prey for raptors, especially bald eagles. The eagle population has increased over the past several decades in parallel with that of the geese. A record number of 476 eagles was observed on the refuge in 2001.

During the first full weekend of December, when eagle numbers are likely to be near their maximum, Eagle Days are celebrated at Squaw Creek. It is not uncommon then to see more than one hundred bald eagles during a single trip around the refuge's nine-mile perimeter road. Some might be perched on tall cottonwoods near the road but are more likely to be standing on muskrat "houses" in the middle of the marsh. Often an eagle will take flight and fly above the massed geese, causing a pandemonium and offering the eagle an opportunity to detect any birds that are weak fliers or are otherwise vulnerable. Eagles in adult plumage cause more panic than do immature birds lacking white heads and tails, suggesting that the geese recognize that adults pose a greater risk than do young ones, which tend to be scavengers rather than effective predators. After the species had recovered from the pesticide poisonings of the mid-1900s, bald eagles first nested successfully at the refuge in 1997. They have since been regular breeders, with two nests usually active.

Many other raptors migrate through the area each fall, especially the slow-flying and soaring hawks called buteos, which use updrafts from the slopes of the loess hills to gain lift for their flight south. The most common buteos are red-tailed hawks, which among counts farther north in southern Iowa compose about 40 percent of the raptors, and are likely to winter not much farther south than Oklahoma and Arkansas. A small percentage of these are dark-plumaged (Harlan's race) red-tails, which have probably migrated from the Yukon drainage of northwestern Canada or Alaska, but the majority of birds are more likely to consist of more extensively white-plumaged individuals (eastern race) coming out of southern Canada and the northern states.

Among the buteo hawks, Swainson's hawks are probably second only in number to red-tails and are very early fall migrants. They usually migrate in large flocks while on their way to southern South America, a trip of about eight thousand miles from central Canada and one that may require more than two months. Turkey vultures are also very common early migrants and closely follow the hilly eastern edge of the river valley for maximum soaring efficiency. Turkey vultures banded in Kansas are known to have migrated as far as northern South America.

Several trends in waterfowl numbers have been evident in recent years at Squaw Creek. Other geese, including Canada geese and greater white-fronted geese, are now common. Like the snow goose, the Canada goose has been increasing nationally for several decades, at least in part because of a greatly expanded food source provided by intensive Great Plains corn farming. Until about the year 2000, maximum numbers of Canada and white-fronted geese on the refuge rarely exceeded a thousand each, but between 2008 and 2010 maximum numbers of Canada geese averaged about fifteen thousand, and those of greater white-fronts averaged about sixteen thousand.

Squaw Creek also attracts great numbers of migrant ducks. Mallards are the most abundant, with maximum 2008–11 numbers ranging between nearly 13,000 to nearly 102,000, the numbers usually peaking in late November. Northern pintails have a migration schedule similar to mallards, with peak yearly populations of about 7,000 to 33,000. Green-winged teal are also late fall and early spring migrants; their 2008–11 peak numbers have ranged from about 3,000 to 17,000. Blue-winged teal are abundant early fall migrants, with peak recent populations of about 3,000 to 20,000. Northern shovelers and gadwalls are the most common of the other surface-feeding ducks, with recent maximum yearly numbers ranging up to about 18,000 and 24,000 birds, respectively. The only relatively common diving duck using the refuge is the gradually increasing ring-necked duck, whose yearly maximum numbers have recently reached as high as 25,000 birds.

As part of an international effort to increase the population of the once-endangered trumpeter swan, several Canadian provinces and northern states have started trumpeter swan reintroduction programs. These efforts have been highly successful, and now this world's most magnificent and largest swan can be seen in many parts of the northern Great Plains. First noted at Squaw Creek in 2000, trumpeter swans have been present with increasing regularity and numbers. The maximum number seen in 2008 was 78, but between 2009 and 2011 a peak average of 148 trumpeter swans were present. The adults and newly fledged young arrive in early fall and usually reach peak numbers by early December or early spring. A few somewhat smaller tundra swans on their way to Atlantic coast wintering areas are sometimes also seen among the trumpeters.

Shorebird migrations at Squaw Creek are also impressive. Species that are common to abundant during both spring and fall include the killdeer; lesser yellowlegs; and the spotted, semipalmated, and least sandpipers. During spring, the semipalmated plover; greater yellowlegs; long-billed dowitcher; and white-rumped, Baird's, and pectoral sandpipers are all common. Many of these species use very different fall migration routes and are much less common then.

Other notable water-dependent birds using the refuge include the American coot, common gallinule, and the Virginia and king rails, all of which have been found to be nesting. Additional wading birds reportedly nesting include the American bittern, least bittern, cattle egret, green heron, and the yellow-crowned and black-crowned night-herons. Great blue herons, great egrets, snowy egrets, and little blue herons are also regularly seen.

All told, at least 310 bird species have been documented or less formally reported on the refuge. This total places the refuge among the most bird-rich locations in the upper Great Plains region and represents the largest number of bird species reported from any national wildlife refuge in Missouri.

Squaw Creek NWR offers a small reflection of what the Missouri valley's wildlife might have resembled during Lewis and Clark's era. The refuge is open sunrise to sunset daily and has a modern interpretive center that is open weekdays all year, and also on weekends during migration periods. Information is available from the refuge headquarters: P.O. Box 158, Mound City, MO 64470; phone 660-442-3187.

References

Johnsgard, P. A. 2012. Squaw Creek National Wildlife Refuge: Gem of the Missouri Valley. *Prairie Fire*, November 2012, pp. 12–13. http://www.prairiefirenewspaper.com/2012/11/ squaw-creek-national-wildlife-refuge-gem-of-the-missouri-valley

10

The Hutton Niobrara Ranch Audubon Nature Sanctuary

Over the first sixty-mile segment of the Niobrara National Scenic and Recreational River, the river makes a graceful bend south, reaching its southernmost point along the northern border of Rock County. There, about twelve miles northeast of Bassett, a new Audubon wildlife sanctuary is situated, like a green emerald set dangling below the blue necklace that is the Niobrara.

The sanctuary, nearly five thousand acres in expanse, is the remarkable gift of the late Harold Hutton, son of a prominent multi-generational homesteading family and a rancher, author, and entrepreneur. Harold was also a lover of nature and decided that he would like to have his land preserved as a nature sanctuary after his death. He initially approached the National Audubon Society, which proved to be unwilling to promise that the land might not be ultimately sold. Luckily, Harold found a willing and interested listener in the form of Ron Klataske, executive director of Audubon of Kansas.

Ron Klataske first met Harold Hutton in 1980, while Klataske was serving as a regional vice president for the National Audubon Society and helping to establish a strategy to win Congressional approval for naming a 76-mile stretch of the middle Niobrara as a national scenic river. This designation would insure that its remarkable geological, paleontological, and ecological treasures would not be destroyed by the impoundment of the valley by a proposed $200-million dam and diversion to be built near Norden. The Norden Dam was part of an envisioned "reclamation" project that would have benefited only a few agricultural interests at the expense of the regional destruction of Nebraska's most unique and most beautiful river.

Fortunately, the Norden Dam project was eventually abandoned, the national scenic river designation was congressionally approved, and the bonds of friendship that had been formed between Klataske and Hutton persisted. After Harold's death, his widow, Lucille, requested that Audubon of Kansas accept the title and stewardship responsibility for the land. It was not until 2008 that the last legal obstacle to the property's grazing leases were settled, and the slow process of habitat restoration could begin.

I was part of an informal delegation representing *Prairie Fire* that visited the sanctuary in May 2014. Four of us spent nearly three days roaming the grasslands, woods, and wet meadows, and trying to absorb the rich diversity of plant and animal life. A sharp-tailed grouse lek, with more than twenty participating males, was located on a grassy hilltop only a half mile from the beautiful guesthouse (Hutton's last home) where we slept, and from which we could hear the birds' daily dawn dances.

From the guesthouse's kitchen windows I watched and photographed many of the bird species attracted to the honeysuckle shrubs and backyard feeders, such as spotted towhee, blue grosbeak, black-capped chickadee, yellow warbler, and northern bobwhite. Turkey vultures patrolled the prairie beyond, and dozens of barn swallows swarmed around the nearby dilapidated barn like excited bees. Two gigantic cottonwoods immediately north of the house hosted probable nesting pairs of red-headed woodpeckers and northern flickers as well as a possible pair of American kestrels. In the past, wood ducks have also nested in the trees' numerous cavities. The porch on the east side of the house had an eastern phoebe nest with a resident incubating female, who was repeatedly frustrated by the frequent human disturbances she had to endure.

One of the two cottonwoods, a three-trunk giant, towered over the other. I decided to roughly estimate its circumference by seeing how many of my fingertip-to-fingertip units of personal measurement (about 80 inches, here defined as one "johnsgard") were needed to circumscribe it. I found that the distance was in excess of six johnsgards, or about 40 feet! What a rich history that tree has no doubt had, and what wonderful animal guests it must have hosted within its cavities and under its leafy canopy over the past century or so.

Along the sanctuary's sandy upland roads I saw uncountable lark sparrows, eastern and western kingbirds, western meadowlarks and mourning doves, dozens of grasshopper sparrows and upland sandpipers, as well as a few long-billed curlews, northern bobwhites, and sharp-tailed grouse. White-tailed deer periodically bounded over the rich Sandhills prairie, and a lone, apparently lost, male bison plodded peacefully past us on his way down a sandy trail toward some destination known only to him. A colony of black-tailed prairie dogs was thriving within a well-fenced boundary, with at least five families present. Ron had skillfully managed to negotiate the Nebraska Game and Parks Commission to allow him to reestablish this colony on the property and exhibit the animals for their educational values and scientific significance. The commissioners' nineteenth-century policies toward prairie dogs are purely political and an absurd failure to recognize the ecological values of this native keystone species. We saw at least four babies peering out of burrow openings that had been protected with heavy iron grating to keep out badgers.

The road down to the river bottom wetlands was rich in scenic beauty and biological diversity. Nearly all the trees, other than the invasive red-cedars, were deciduous hardwoods, especially plains cottonwood, but there was also green ash, boxelder, and various eastern woodland shrubs, such as red osier dogwood, wolfberry, and chokecherry. A few ponderosa pines are present on the sanctuary's property and are probably the easternmost naturally occurring ponderosas on the south side of the Niobrara Valley. A grove of mature bur oaks surrounds the original homestead site, where a beautiful wood-frame house that had been built in 1903 and had replaced an earlier log cabin still stands, as does a precariously tilting outhouse. The house's fate remains to be determined, although the outhouse is now probably acceptable only to porcupines and eastern woodrats, which don't seem to object to its sloping seats.

The bottomlands had several meadows supporting territorial bobolinks and red-winged blackbirds as well as a few yellow-headed blackbirds, whose squeaking courtship calls sounded like so many rusty gates. Sandhill cranes have nested and produced young in at least one of the marsh meadows during the past few years, representing perhaps the first record of sandhill cranes breeding in northern Nebraska since the late 1800s. Virginia rails have been heard calling from the phragmites marsh, and we flushed a lone great blue heron.

One evening we heard whip-poor-wills, an eastern forest species near the western edge of its range, calling in an oak grove. We also heard yellow-breasted chats calling in the riverine woods; this now mostly western species has nearly disappeared from eastern Nebraska, so its occurrence so far east is noteworthy. The orioles here appear to be of the eastern (Baltimore) species rather than the western-oriented Bullock's oriole. Likewise, the bunting here is reportedly the eastern indigo bunting, rather than the western lazuli bunting, whereas the resident grosbeak is evidently the western black-headed species rather than the eastern rose-breasted type. All of these species-pairs sometimes hybridize in the Niobrara valley, as do the yellow- and red-shafted forms of the northern flicker. Both eastern and western meadowlarks have also been reported from Rock County, further illustrating this region's transitional biogeographic nature.

Along the river's edge we could see evidence of beaver activity, and river otters have also been observed here. Farther out on the river a flock of nonbreeding Canada geese was gathered, and several pairs were scattered over the meadows where they could fight over territorial boundaries. Male bobolinks resembling feathery flowers while perched on taller plants periodically erupted from the meadow into their melodic song flights, and on the adjacent hillside nearly a dozen wild turkeys were clustered, preoccupied with their own equally spectacular mating rituals.

After a long afternoon of hiking and birding, our last sunset was spent on an overlook that provides both upstream and downstream vistas for a mile or more. Looking upstream, the river is notably wide

and shallow, with many bare sandy islands of varied artistic configu-
rations. As we stood there, silently watching the daylight turn softly
into twilight, and the sky colors slowly burn out into shades of gray,
the unison calls of two sandhill cranes suddenly broke the silence and
echoed down the valley. I felt the goose bumps form on my arms as
my favorite and the most emotionally powerful sound in the world
suddenly penetrated my consciousness; it reminded me yet again why
Nebraska is my one and only true spiritual home.

References

Johnsgard, P. A. 2014. Hutton Niobrara Ranch Wildlife Sanctuary.
Prairie Fire, July 2014, pp. 12–14. http://www.prairiefirenewspaper.
com/2014/07/hutton-niobrara-ranch-wildlife-sanctuary

11

Yellowstone National Park:
A Personal History

My first view of Yellowstone National Park occurred when I was a teenager, just after World War II, when gas was again becoming easily available and my father had purchased a 1946 Ford. I had pleaded with my parents to consider a vacation trip to visit Yellowstone Park for our annual vacation; I even threatened to hitchhike there, if necessary. I had just purchased my first 35mm camera, an Argus C-3, which was totally unsuited for photographing wildlife but which I felt would at least be adequate for scenic photography.

My dearest wishes were realized when my parents agreed to the trip, and we set off in late June, driving via South Dakota's Black Hills and Wyoming's Bighorn Mountains. These regions provided my first views of real mountains, which were soon outmatched by the amazing alpine scenery we encountered as we approached the park on the Beartooth Highway. We spent two days in the park, the most memorable aspect of which for me was the amazing number of black bears that we saw. We counted well over fifty within the park, including several females with cubs, as well as bison, elk, and mule deer, plus a lone coyote. I saw dozens of bird species for the first time, such as Steller's jays, gray jays, and Clark's nutcrackers, and had a fleeting but memorable glimpse of a rare Lewis's woodpecker. I also vividly remember seeing ospreys nesting on rocky pinnacles in Yellowstone Canyon.

That trip caused me to fall in love with the Rocky Mountains, and thereafter my dreams always pointed westward. Following graduate work in the state of Washington, and later graduate and postdoctoral studies in New York and England, I and my own family settled in Nebraska, only a day's drive from the Wyoming mountains. Thereafter I spent many summers teaching ornithology in western Nebraska, with occasional field trips to Rocky Mountain National Park, but the Yellowstone region kept calling me. That itch was finally satisfied when I received a small grant from the New York Zoological Society to spend two summers (1975 and 1976) at the Jackson Hole Biological Station in Grand Teton National Park. On my grant application I stated that I would study the breeding behavior of sandhill cranes, but after my arrival I soon was also being absorbed by watching such wonderful birds as trumpeter swans, prairie falcons, common ravens, and calliope hummingbirds, and mammals such as pine martens, moose, elk, and coyotes. While there, my ex-student Tom Mangelsen visited me for about a week, camping out at the Jenny Lake campground. He soon thereafter decided to move to Jackson Hole and began assembling an amazing portfolio of wildlife photos that would identify him as one of the premier wildlife photographers of the world.

After my far-too-short summers in the Tetons had passed, I sat down to write a book about my experiences. But, after writing nine chapters in fairly rapid succession, I hit a writer's block and couldn't think of how to put together a satisfying ending. The manuscript then sat unfinished for several years, until one day I just decided I would simply try to tie up the loose ends of the varied stories and make a brief summation. That done, I drew about a dozen pen-and-ink drawings, assembled some photos and sent them off to a university press editor whom I had met in the Tetons. My book, *Teton Wildlife: Observations by a Naturalist*, appeared in 1982.

Tom Mangelsen and I have remained close friends for more than forty years, and he has often let me use one of his photos for book jacket covers. Given Tom's love for Jackson Hole, I wasn't surprised when, after I proposed doing a joint book project one March day in 2010, he suggested that it be on the Greater Yellowstone region. Writing a book on the vast Greater Yellowstone ecosystem of northwestern Wyoming gave me an excuse to return to the region in 2012, nearly forty years after my earlier research there. In the interim, major forest fires had occurred in Yellowstone Park, and the biological station had been moved from a relatively vulnerable site directly below the aging Jackson Lake dam to a scenic location along the shoreline of Jackson Lake.

One of my most favorite sites, a marshy pond near Rockefeller Lodge that for about three decades had supported a pair of trumpeter swans, had nearly dried up. Sadly, some dear friends such as "Mardy" Murie, the region's beloved symbol of wilderness conservation, had passed on, but the wildlife that she cherished had barely changed. The sandhill cranes still were using their traditional territories, ospreys were still nesting on rocky pinnacles in Yellowstone Canyon, ravens were still panhandling at tourist stops, and the woodland flowers were as beautiful as ever. However, the chances of seeing black bears were almost nil, owing to a park policy of bear population control designed to reduce the number of dangerous interactions between humans and bears.

Since the fires of the 1980s, there has been a substantial regrowth of lodgepole pines below the charred remains of the previous centuries-old forest; the fires had caused the resin-coated lodgepole cones to burst open and release their long-held seeds into the newly mineral-enriched soil. A riot of colorful wildflowers, especially fireweed, now often carpet the regenerating woodland floor. Among the other changes to Yellowstone has been the reintroduction of wolves, which had been eliminated from the park in the 1920s. The resulting changes in the ecology of the elk and other large mammals, and the impact of the wolf-thinned elk population on the growth of aspens and other important food plants for large mammals have been substantial, and have also resulted in a smaller but healthier elk population. The Grand Teton's bison population has exploded, from a captive herd of a few dozen in the 1970s to a freely ranging herd of about nine hundred animals that are being legally culled by sport hunters whenever they stray from the boundaries of the national park, just as any wolves that happen to leave park boundaries are likely to be shot on sight. Nevertheless, visitors to Yellowstone and Grand Teton parks now have the possibility of not only seeing wild wolves but also a slight chance of seeing grizzly bears.

Both the trumpeter swan and sandhill crane populations have increased in Yellowstone Park since the 1970s, and the same is probably true of the osprey and bald eagle. Rather sadly, perhaps the greatest obvious change in Yellowstone in the past half-century has been the parallel increase in park visitors. Camping sites must be reserved weeks, if not months, in advance. In 2012 Yellowstone National Park had 3.4 million visitors, as compared with 2.5 million in 1976, and 800,000 when I first visited in 1946. During the 1940s, the narrow, winding roads were no problem; the major factors then tending to hold up traffic flow were occasional "bear jams" caused by people stopping to photograph, or even hand-feed, bears along the roadsides. Now those same mountain roads must endure the effects of a million or more cars in a single year, and traffic jams lasting a half hour or more, resulting from the sightings of a bear, wolf, or even a coyote, are likely to cause frayed nerves and accidents. When I was last in Yellowstone, an impatient driver decided to bypass a bear jam by recklessly driving off the road and hitting a mother grizzly bear. The bear had to be put down, and the cubs had to be captured for zoo rearing. If ever a national park was in danger of being loved to death, Yellowstone is a prime example.

Yet, for all the tourists and delays, it is not hard to park your car, find a hiking trail, and soon be immersed in the magic of the place and the moment. The things I most loved about Yellowstone as a youngster are still there; it is now only slightly harder to find them. The persistence of unmodified nature remnants and the natural processes that are still present in national parks are chief among their glories. And to be able to show your children or grandchildren examples of your own dearest memories, such as visiting Old Faithful with your parents or seeing and hearing a wild elk on a mountain slope, is one of the great joys of life, and among the many reasons we must cherish and pass on to following generations these marvelous symbols of a wild and pristine America.

References

Johnsgard, P. A. 2013. *Yellowstone Wildlife: Ecology and Natural History of the Greater Yellowstone Ecosystem.* (Photographs by Thomas D. Mangelsen.) Boulder: University Press of Colorado. 228 pp.

Johnsgard, P. A. 2013. A Yellowstone story. *Prairie Fire,* August 2013, pp. 1, 3, 4. http://www.prairiefirenewspaper.com/2013/08/a-yellowstone-story

Grizzly bear

PART III

Conservation in the Great Plains
and Rocky Mountains

Mountain lion

12

To Kill a Mountain Lion

In 1987, to celebrate my survival of a serious heart attack, my older brother Keith suggested to me that we go to Africa on a photo safari, something both of us had dreamed of doing for much of our lives but had never acted on. Although my own primary interest was birding and his was in climbing Mt. Kenya, we both especially looked forward to seeing such wonderful megafauna as elephants, cheetahs, and lions. While there, we spent a good deal of time watching a lion pride on the Serengeti and were greatly impressed by the bravery of young Maasai men, who spent the daylight hours guarding their cattle from lion attacks armed only with a spear. Indeed, the ultimate and sometimes fatal bravery test of a Maasai warrior is to kill a lion with nothing more than his spear.

Keith was so taken by the history and beauty of some of these museum-piece spears that he purchased two of them from some Maasai whom we encountered while crossing the Serengeti. I was very disappointed in his decision because these weapons were no doubt heirlooms that had been passed down through many familial generations. Although they could probably be replaced by modern and perhaps even better factory-made versions, I felt that such exchanges result in a cheapening of the Maasai culture, as was the then-common tendency for tourists to trade transistor radios or baseball caps for beadwork and other aboriginal souvenirs.

When we returned home, Keith proudly put his Maasai spears and related artifacts on display in his house, in essentially the same way that big-game hunters often return home with the trophy heads of animals that they have shot in Africa. It is possible that displaying the horns, antlers, tusks, and other secondary sexual characteristics of these magnificent animals may help boost the ego of dedicated nimrods. However, killing large animals at a great distance and with a high-powered rifle is hardly comparable to the invisible badge of courage that Maasai men exhibit every time they face a threatening lion while holding nothing but a handmade and metal-tipped wooden spear. Tom Mangelsen, Nebraska's internationally known wildlife photographer, conservationist, and founder of the nonprofit Cougar Fund, has informed me that since lions are now becoming quite rare on the Serengeti, there has been a big awareness campaign with the Maasai that they no longer kill lions in order to become a recognized warrior or reach manhood.

In Nebraska, we are now beginning to enjoy the occasional presence of mountain lions (also called cougars, pumas, and catamounts), which had been absent in the state for a century and are now increasingly reappearing. After being extirpated from the central Great Plains by 1891, mountain lions were not again sighted in Nebraska until 1991. Since then, more than one hundred confirmed sightings have been made in the state outside of the Pine Ridge, and it is believed that a population of twenty-two to twenty-four animals exists in the Pine Ridge region of Sioux, Dawes, and Sheridan counties. Those individuals appearing elsewhere are mostly young animals that have been forced out of their Pine Ridge and Black Hills homeland as a result of competition from older animals. They have been seen crossing the state along such natural corridors as the Niobrara, Loup, and Platte rivers, very rarely encountering humans, but posing imagined threats during such encounters.

Mountain lions are primarily predators on deer in their usual habitats, and the older animals are sufficiently wary of humans to remain well away from any human contacts. In balanced populations, the mountain lions keep the deer population in check and selectively eliminate sick or weakened individuals. It is the young, inexperienced lions, driven out of the territories of older individuals, that are most likely to wander into strange places and begin selecting easily obtained prey, such as domesticated livestock, pets, and, extremely rarely, people.

During the century-long period 1890–1990, only fifty-three attacks on humans by mountain lions were documented throughout the United States and Canada, ten of which were fatal. From 1991 to the present, nine additional fatal attacks have occurred, including four in California, three in western Canada, and two in Colorado. By comparison, 34,000 people were killed in the United States by vehicular accidents in 2012, and an average of about 32,000 die annually from firearms. The probability of being killed in an auto accident or being killed by gunshot (most often by a family member or other acquaintance) is thus more than a thousand times greater than being attacked by a mountain lion over one's entire life, even assuming a lifetime of one hundred years.

The recent increase in human-lion encounters is in part a reflection of increasing human populations and ever-greater access by humans into lion country by hikers, bicyclists, and campers. The combination of decreasing lion habitat and increasing pressures on immature lions to spread into marginal areas has only increased the likelihood of contacts. Sport hunting is another factor that undesirably influences interactions between mountain lions and humans.

To kill a mountain lion is disgustingly simple. A common method is to use professional guides whose dogs have attached radio telemetry units. When the dogs have found and chased a mountain lion into a tree, it is necessary only to approach the tree and, with a .22 or other small-caliber pistol (so as not to damage the pelt too badly), shoot it out of the tree. Using a small-caliber gun only prolongs the death of the animal but no doubt allows for a more elaborate recounting of the hunt. As Nebraska's Senator Ernie Chambers has bluntly remarked, "That's not hunting, that's slaughter." Killing adult mountain lions often has other serious consequences. The loss of a mother with dependent young is also a sentence of death by starvation for the kittens, something a trophy hunter is probably unlikely to think about as he visualizes another hide to be nailed to the wall.

Of the twelve western states with viable breeding populations, most have regulated hunting seasons. As might be expected, Texas allows unlimited hunting of mountain lions, whereas California has recognized them as an intrinsic part of the state's natural heritage and has classified them a protected species since 1990. The state of Washington limits the kill to the species' biological rate of increase, estimated at no more than 14 percent. In Nebraska only a single case of breeding has so far been documented.

A thriving mountain lion population in Nebraska would help limit our out-of-control deer population. There were more than 2,500 deer-car collisions in Nebraska in 2012, resulting in three human fatalities, so deer are millions of times more hazardous to both the property and health of Nebraskans than are mountain lions. Deer also host the ticks that most often transmit Lyme disease. More than thirty thousand cases of this chronic and often-crippling disease are reported annually, according to the national Centers for Disease Control and Prevention, and more than fifty confirmed cases have occurred in Nebraska since 2003. Considering their influence as primary deer predators and thus helping to reduce the incidence of deer-car accidents and Lyme disease, mountain lions must be regarded as one of the most beneficial of Nebraska's wildlife. Yet, a still-uncertain number have been killed for various, often questionable, reasons since they first reappeared in the state in 1991.

Research by biologists in Washington has shown that heavy hunting pressure on cougars often forces young individuals into the fringes of suitable habitat, increasingly exposing them to humans. Research there has shown that hunting also results in more frequent conflicts with people. Nevertheless, the Nebraska Game and Parks Commission decided to open the state's first hunting season on mountain lions in 2014, even though they are far more rare in Nebraska than are some of our nationally endangered or threatened species, such as least terns.

Rather than considering all the undesirable effects of mountain lion hunting just mentioned, the Game and Parks Commission crafted a set of regulations designed to bring the maximum amount of revenue into the agency. Two people were to be chosen to hunt in the Pine Ridge unit of the Nebraska National Forest between January 1 and February 14, 2014, and both were allowed to kill a lion with the help of tracking dogs. One of the two permit holders was to be chosen by lottery, and the other was determined by a banquet auction, which netted the Game and Parks Commission $13,500, in addition to the banquet profits.

An additional one hundred hunters were also chosen by lottery for opportunities to buy permits to hunt in the Pine Ridge counties from February 15 to March 31, with a maximum total kill of two lions. There is no overall limit on the number of permits sold or lions killed over most of the rest of the state (the "prairie hunting unit") and throughout the rest of the year. Nearly four hundred permits were issued. Only one lion kill was allowed per hunter, and, although they would no doubt make cute trophies, shooting kittens was not allowed.

Within two days of the start of January, both permit holders had killed their allotted animals. The lottery was won by a teenager who had initially killed a mountain lion when he was only thirteen years old, and who said he "felt great" about his most recent success. The auction winner killed a 138-pound male, thus paying about $100 per pound for the legal right to eliminate one of these magnificent animals. He had killed two mountain lions previously and already had 150 trophy mounts in his home. Presumably he needed yet another. Later, an adult female was legally killed for sport on February 26, 2014, in Sioux County, ending the second phase of legal hunting in the Pine Ridge. An adult male was later legally shot by a hunter on October 5, in Knox County, part of the almost statewide hunting unit.

An adult male was accidentally killed by a vehicle on February 1, 2014, in Sioux County, and an adult was killed by a cable entanglement in Custer County on February 16. Another young male was shot on March 21 when it was seen "threatening" a chicken coop in Sheridan County. In June an adult was caught in a trap set sometime in Sioux County. The trap had been left unattended by federal trappers from the USDA Animal and Plant Health Inspection Service, APHIS (the friendly government folks who will shoot, trap, or poison nearly any animal that farmers and ranchers find annoying), leaving the doomed animal to die in agony. Its decaying carcass was not found until early July. A young female was illegally shot near Chadron, Sioux County, July 19, and a lactating female was illegally shot by a hunter in early September, in Sioux County. Her kittens were not found and no doubt starved. Another adult female was killed by a vehicle in Wheeler County on October 9, and a subadult female was killed by a rancher in Dawes County on October 27.

According to a Game and Parks Commission report of October 23, 2014, eleven known mountain lion deaths from all causes had been documented during the previous 365 days in the Pine Ridge region alone. This estimate brought the statewide 2014 death total to at least fourteen, not counting the unknown number of kittens of the female killed in September. The high number of deaths attributed to causes other than hunting makes it clear that sport hunting is not a feasible method of managing the tiny population of mountain lions in Nebraska. At the end of the year, the Game and Parks Commission announced that there would not be another hunting season for mountain lions until the situation had been further researched.

References

Busch, R. H. 1996. *The Cougar Almanac: A Complete Natural History of the American Mountain Lion.* New York: Lyons & Burford.

Chadwick, D. 2013. Ghost cats. *National Geographic Magazine* 224(6):64–82.

Johnsgard, P. A. 2014. To kill a mountain lion. *Prairie Fire,* January 2014, pp. 18–19. http://www.prairiefirenewspaper.com/2014/02/to-kill-a-mountain-lion

Mangelsen, T. D., and C. S. Blessley. 2000. *Spirit of the Rockies: The Mountain Lions of Jackson Hole.* Omaha, NE: Images of Nature.

13

The Lives and Deaths of Yellowstone's Grizzlies

About fifty thousand years ago, as the northern hemisphere was locked in a global deep-freeze and the continental glaciers of the Pleistocene were at a maximum, a large land bridge that connected Asia and North America existed in the general region now occupied by the Bering Sea and Alaska, the so-called Beringia region. Across that corridor many mammals migrated from Asia over the millennia, including North America's ancestral brown bears and, much more recently, the first humans. One early influx of bears arrived in North America from Asia less than fifty thousand years ago. Some of these ancestral Alaskan brown bears apparently became isolated in island and coastal habitats by the last of the great glaciers, and the polar bear evolved from them. A later influx of bears from Asia produced the modern brown and grizzly bears (*Ursus arctos*).

These were not the first American bears. As early as seven million years ago, several bear species were already present in North America. The largest mid-Pleistocene bear was the giant short-faced bear. This behemoth probably reached weights in excess of two thousand pounds, or nearly three times the average size of a modern grizzly, and it was perhaps able to subdue some of the largest of Pleistocene mammals. This bear and its contemporary relatives, such as the cave bear, eventually became extinct, except for one surviving descendant, the South American spectacled bear. A much smaller bear that had evolved in the Old World about 1.5 million years ago and arrived at least eight thousand years ago in North America became the modern black bear (*Ursus americanus*).

From their original area of North American occupation in

89

Beringia, the ancestral brown bears moved south into central North America toward the end of the Pleistocene, or about twenty thousand years ago. At their peak, their range extended south into northern Mexico, and east to the edge of the prairies in Canada's Prairie Provinces and the Great Plains states. In Alaska, these huge bears are called Alaska brown bears, or are sometimes known as Kodiak bears. They weigh on average up to a third more than the more southern populations and can rarely exceed one thousand pounds. The generally accepted name for the populations south of Canada is grizzly bear, in reference to the adults' gray-tipped ("grizzled") pelage. Transitional populations link these two extreme genetic types and even a few recent hybrids between Alaskan brown bears and polar bears.

During presettlement times, the grizzly was widespread in western North America, from the Cascade and Sierra Nevada mountains east across the Rocky Mountains to the high plains grasslands. During 1804–5, grizzlies were encountered by the Lewis and Clark expedition in what is now North Dakota and Montana, and were seen again by Clark on his return trip down the Yellowstone River in 1806. The group's narratives of meeting grizzly bears, which they variously called white bears or gray bears, still provide for exciting reading material. Clark's account of chasing a grizzly for two miles while on horseback provides the first evidence of grizzlies in the greater Yellowstone ecosystem.

More recently, as firearms and ammunition have improved, killing a grizzly bear as a unique hunter's trophy has increasingly become one of the ultimate icons of manhood for the most thoroughly gun-addicted Americans. As a result, nearly all the grizzly populations of western North America have been extirpated, except in remote areas such as Alaska, and within a few well-monitored sanctuaries such as our western national parks.

With the 1973 passage of the Endangered Species Act, the grizzly bear was classified as a threatened species throughout the lower forty-eight states. In a corollary action, and while I was doing field research in the Tetons, the greater Yellowstone region was proposed as critical habitat for grizzlies in 1976. This recommendation initiated nearly as much anger among ranchers, landowners, and developers as do current federal attempts to impose national jurisdiction over so-called states' rights. As a result of these pressures, the critical habitat designation for Yellowstone was never officially adopted.

Since Yellowstone National Park's formation in 1872, its bears theoretically have been secure because, according to its official 1883 management principles, the only animals that can be legally killed within park boundaries are fish. However, the park's principals have rarely followed these principles. For example, to satisfy fishermen, park personnel regularly destroyed the eggs in a nesting colony of American white pelicans on a small island in Yellowstone Lake, although white pelicans consume almost no fish of sporting value. Until the early decades of the twentieth century, thousands of coyotes, nearly all of the park's mountain lions, and all of the park's wolves were shot or poisoned. The loss of these predators resulted in large population increases in prey species such as elk, and their overgrazing produced widespread habitat deterioration.

I first saw wild bears on a trip to Yellowstone with my parents during the post-war recovery years of the late 1940s; we observed more than fifty black bears during a memorable two-day trip through the park. My teenage introduction to bears had occurred during the period when roadside feeding of animals by tourists in national parks was the norm. Two decades later, Yellowstone National Park began a campaign to separate bears from all human encounters and dealt harshly with any bears that failed to cooperate.

This draconian policy had its origins in 1967, after two grizzlies in Glacier National Park killed two young women campers. The women had both been wearing perfume, leading park officials to claim that the bears had been attracted to them by odor, rather than the attack being a result of the park's inadequate bear management. At that time, bear feeding by tourists was a well-established practice at both Glacier and Yellowstone parks, and in both locations the animals had lost all fear of humans.

The two deaths in Glacier represented only the fourth and fifth lethal attacks by grizzlies on humans in the entire history of the national parks, but it caused the administrators of national parks to reevaluate their bear policy. Yellowstone Park modified its garbage dumps by eliminating anything that might be attractive to bears. This change forced the bears to search elsewhere for food, such as around campgrounds. During 1966, before the garbage dump policy took effect, a total of nine bears that visited a campground near Yellowstone Lake were trapped and removed or killed. In 1968, after a nearby dump had eliminated all access to garbage by bears, the number of them removed or killed there had risen almost four fold to thirty-three.

Accurate estimates of bear mortality associated with Yellowstone's control actions are impossible to obtain. For example, in the thirteen years between 1970 and 1982, Yellowstone officials reported an average annual loss of eighteen grizzly bears that died accidentally, were trapped and euthanized, or were transported to remote locations. However, Frank Craighead reported in his 1979 *Track of the Grizzly* that over the four-year period 1969–72 an average of thirty-two Yellowstone grizzlies were killed annually.

In 1971 alone, well over forty grizzlies were killed near the wild-west town of West Yellowstone, located just outside the western boundary of Yellowstone Park, where snowmobiles have priority over cars and owning lots of firearms is a status symbol. The grizzly deaths included eighteen radio-tagged bears that had been part of the Craighead brothers' long-term and monumental study on Yellowstone's grizzly populations and ecology. Park officials did not receive the Craigheads' research results well and tried hard to restrict or terminate their studies.

A 1975 National Academy of Sciences report estimated a greater Yellowstone population of about three hundred grizzlies, a total that was lowered by a team of independent scientists to possibly fewer than two hundred by 1982. By then the Park Service had reassessed and reduced its control activities. It is also becoming increasingly apparent that, because of the very large home ranges of grizzlies, illegal killing of the animals outside the park strongly influences regional bear numbers. Grizzly pelts and other body parts, such as their claws, have high commercial value, making the bears attractive targets for poachers.

In recent decades the regional prospects for grizzlies have improved through better-informed park management and slightly improved control of illegal killings. However, in 2012 a record number of fifty-six bears were known to have been killed by humans in the greater Yellowstone region, representing about 10 percent of their estimated total population. By comparison, a total of seven human deaths have been caused by Yellowstone's grizzlies during the park's entire 142-year history. Glacier National Park has likewise had seven lethal grizzly attacks over its 104-year history. Yellowstone Park averages well over 3 million visitors per year, and Glacier slightly under 2 million, so the chances of being killed by a bear at either park are much less likely than of becoming an astronaut.

By comparison, Yellowstone typically has up to ten bison attacks on humans per year, and during the fifteen years from 1979 to 1994 there were two fatalities and fifty-six injuries caused by bison in Yellowstone Park. Thus, the park's seemingly tame and lethargic bison are hundreds of times more likely to attack visitors than are its grizzly bears. (I write from personal experience, having been chased and very nearly trampled by a rutting male bison in the Black Hills during the 1980s.) Closer to home, domestic dogs and cattle each kill an average of roughly twenty Americans annually, while bees, hornets, and wasps average more than sixty.

Yellowstone's grizzly populations have markedly improved lately, in spite of high cub mortality rates and an undisclosed number of bears being euthanized by the park. Of seven females with cubs that a friend monitored in 2013, only two still had any yearlings present in 2014. The bears' regional annual growth rate from 1983 to 2001 has been estimated at 4 percent to 7 percent, and James Halfpenny estimated in his 2007 *Yellowstone Bears in the Wild* that the greater Yellowstone ecosystem then held five hundred to six hundred grizzly bears. Grizzlies have also recently expanded their ranges south out of

Yellowstone into Grand Teton National Park, where visitors are now increasingly likely to see them.

In September 2013 I visited Grand Teton National Park and with Tom Mangelsen saw many of the places I had come to love during the 1970s. There were many obvious changes. For example, the Teton bison herd, which had consisted of a few dozen animals when I first saw it in the 1940s, had multiplied to nearly 1,000 head, and Yellowstone Park had about 3,500.

Besides seeing all the common Teton birds and mammals, Tom and I also extensively watched three subadult grizzly bears peacefully foraging on plant roots in grassy subalpine meadows near Togwotee Lodge. The bears also scavenged the carcass of a moose that a trophy hunter had killed and left behind all but the head and antlers to rot. Fall grizzly foods in the Yellowstone area often consist mostly of the seeds of whitebark pines dug out of squirrel caches, army cutworm moths, and a wide variety of plant leaves and roots.

For three days Tom and I watched the bears, and at times more than twenty carloads of tourists and local wildlife photographers lined the roadsides. None bothered the bears, and the bears paid little attention to the onlookers. On a few occasions a bear would cross the highway, patiently waiting for the traffic to thin out and provide a safe crossing. One even wandered to within a stone's throw of our parked car, providing me with a heart-stopping sense of awe at seeing such a beautiful animal in its element and imprinting on my mind an incredible lifetime memory.

Tom recently told me that there is now an all-out effort to trap most of Yellowstone's regional grizzlies during this summer and fall. One male (#760) was trapped twice in less than nine months and was fitted with a radio collar. He is one of the few bears that was often seen by park visitors during 2014 and probably has been observed by hundreds of thousands over the past four years. With no history of being aggressive, he nevertheless now conspicuously wears two large yellow ear tags and a big radio collar, reminding a wildlife watcher more of a decorated Christmas tree than a wild bear. As Tom said,

"The American public does not want to come to their national parks to see Christmas-tree bears!"

More ominously, the grizzly will be legally hunted as a trophy species in Wyoming, Idaho, and Montana if it is regionally delisted from its current threatened status, as has been proposed by the U.S. Fish and Wildlife Service. The Wyoming Game and Fish Department already has made plans for a grizzly bear hunt whenever the species is delisted, with permits ("tags") to be sold at a bargain price of $660 each and the possible sale of as many as fifteen permits.

Not all big-game hunters are expert marksmen. More than two hundred years ago, Lewis and Clark learned the extreme dangers of coping with wounded grizzly bears. With that thought in mind, the greater Yellowstone region may soon become a more dangerous place for both bears and humans, and a far sadder one, in which the sight of free-roaming and relatively tame grizzlies will become nothing but a memory.

References

Craighead, F. C. 1979. *Track of the Grizzly*. San Francisco: Sierra Club Books.

Halfpenny, J. C. 2007. *Yellowstone Bears in the Wild*. Helena, MT: Riverbend Publishing.

Johnsgard, P. A. 2013. *Yellowstone Wildlife: Ecology and Natural History of the Greater Yellowstone Ecosystem*. (Photographs by Thomas D. Mangelsen.) Boulder, CO: University Press of Colorado.

Johnsgard, P. A. 2014. The lives and deaths of Yellowstone's grizzlies. *Prairie Fire*, August 2014, pp. 1–3. http://www.prairiefirenewspaper.com/2014/08/the-lives-and-deaths-of-yellowstones-grizzlies

McNamee, T. 1984. *The Grizzly Bear*. New York: Knopf.

14

It's Crane Season—in Wyoming

Considering that Nebraska and Wyoming are adjoining states, it is surprising that the two states' sandhill crane populations are so very different. More than 90 percent of the five hundred thousand–plus sandhills seen annually in Nebraska are migrants of two smaller races (lesser and Canadian) that are present only when they are heading to or coming from breeding areas that may be located up to nearly four thousand miles away. In Wyoming these small sandhill cranes (weighing about six to eight pounds) occur only in the eastern parts of the state, where they migrate through the eastern plains during spring and fall, and are sufficiently abundant in the fall to be considered as legally hunted game birds.

Only a handful of pairs of sandhill cranes annually nest in central and western Nebraska, and these are of the greater race, adults of which often weigh nine to ten pounds. However, throughout many of Wyoming's mountain ranges, and especially in far western Wyoming, greater sandhill cranes are present during summer, breeding in mountain meadows, valley pastures, and middle- to low-altitude wetlands. Nesting sandhill cranes are solitary, remarkably inconspicuous during the nesting season, and probably overlooked by most people. However, a person can easily recognize the species' distinctive loud and memorable bugle-like calls, which can readily be heard over a distance of a half mile or more and are important modes of communication between pairs and families.

During the mid-1970s, I spent two summers in Grand Teton National Park, studying several species of birds and mammals. I was especially interested in sandhill cranes and trumpeter swans, perhaps the park's two most spectacular birds and also among its rarest. Over the entire park, I was able to find a few nesting pairs of each of these species. Both of them often nested in close proximity, especially in and around shallow marshy wetlands produced as a result of beaver dam-building activities. They often also shared them with foraging moose and many other water-related birds, such as Barrow's goldeneyes and red-winged blackbirds.

I was able to study one nesting pair of sandhill cranes unusually well, as its nesting site was located in an area once used as a picnic ground but since abandoned. The only evidence of its past life was a rather decrepit outhouse overlooking a small beaver pond, at the edge of which and about forty yards away was the crane nest. By using the out-house as a blind I was able to avoid setting up a tent blind, which might have caused the adults to desert their nest. I found the nest in early June and visited it every few days. By sitting on the built-in seat, and open-ing the door only far enough to use my binoculars and telephoto lens, I had the most perfect, if not aesthetically ideal, viewing location.

By the time I found the nest, the body plumages of both mem-bers of the pair were already tinted a rich, rusty brown by their mud-spreading and preening behavior, thus altering the bird's silvery gray feather coloration to a hue closely approaching that of dead marsh vegetation. Like sandhill cranes generally, the two birds alternated their incubation duties, periodically changing positions. However, the male more often stood guard some distance from the nest, his head held high and his senses alert to any sights or sounds of approach-ing danger. The female, conspicuous on the rush-built nest, usually incubated with her head also held high. At any sign of danger she would flatten out on the nest and suddenly resemble a large and ob-long brown rock.

The male was quite effective at keeping other birds away from the nest and often actively searched for the nests and eggs of other marsh birds. I saw him once flush a female cinnamon teal from her nest and eat most of her eggs, and on another occasion consume the entire nest contents of a red-winged blackbird. In retaliation the male red-winged blackbird would often approach the male crane from behind and peck at his head or back feathers, but to no avail.

I was lucky enough to be watching when the cranes' first egg hatched, some thirty days after its incubation had begun. Female cranes lay their two eggs one or two days apart and begin incubation immediately. As a result, the eggs don't hatch synchronously, as they do in waterfowl. Hatching of the egg was a slow process, but what finally emerged was a beautiful coppery-gold chick (which crane biologists traditionally call a colt), as shiny as a newly minted penny. For several hours his (actual sex unknown) pink legs were somewhat swollen, and he had a hard time balancing on them. Yet before the day was over he was able to climb up on his mother's back and rest among her warm mantle feathers.

By the next morning the chick had gained enough composure to swim along behind his father, who foraged up to thirty or forty yards from the nest, while the female was still sitting on the nest, waiting for the second egg to hatch.

Being the second chick to hatch is usually bad news for a crane, as the twenty-four- to forty-eight-hour difference in the resulting chick ages makes a great difference in survival probabilities. Unless the two chicks are separated and raised somewhat apart from one another, the two siblings tend to interact aggressively. Although these fights are not fatal, they evidently place enough stress on the younger bird to increase the chances of its mortality.

After the hatching of the second egg, crane parents leave the nest and move into fairly heavy cover, where the young birds become virtually invisible among the taller vegetation. The fledging period, between the time of hatching and first flight, averages somewhat over seventy days in greater sandhill cranes. During that long period of feather and bodily growth in the chick, the adults typically acquire a new set of wing feathers and begin to replace their brown-stained body feathers. Flying competence is acquired slowly, and one of the adults will often take a colt on exercise flights over gradually increasing distances. These flights are probably also useful in teaching young birds local landmarks.

By September the crane population of the Yellowstone-Teton

region begins to flock and gather and prepare for the fall migration. They assemble in the Teton basin, on the Idaho side of the Teton Range, together with post-breeding cranes from farther north, such as the large population nesting around Idaho's Grays Lake National Wildlife Refuge. The flocks then work their way southward. Nine sandhill cranes that were radio tagged in Yellowstone and Grand Teton national parks by Rodney Drewien and his colleagues made a fall staging stopover in the San Luis Valley of southern Colorado, and then moved on south to winter along the middle Rio Grande valley, nearly nine hundred miles south of Yellowstone. All eight of the radio-tagged juveniles left their parents the following spring and summered 2.4 to 37 miles from their natal areas. By their third summer, three of these birds returned to the same areas they had used when they were yearlings, while three others settled 1.8 to 28.7 miles from their natal homes.

The breeding crane population of Wyoming has expanded its range eastward in recent years. An atlas of Wyoming bird distributions that was published in 1992 indicated that then Wyoming had sandhill crane breeding records essentially limited to the western half of Wyoming. Helen Downing, a Bighorn Mountains bird authority, documented only four regional breeding records for sandhill cranes dating back to 1982. Many more breedings in this region have since been documented. These findings suggest a recently increasing and expanding local crane population in the Bighorn region and across the Central Flyway region of eastern Wyoming.

From 1975 to 2012, an average of 16 midcontinent (lesser) sandhill cranes were estimated to have been killed annually by sport hunters in the Central Flyway of eastern Wyoming, while an average of 133 were killed in Wyoming from the Rocky Mountain population of greater sandhills between 1981 and 2010 (Kruse et al., 2010, 2013). This latter population appears to have remained fairly stable, at about 20,000 birds, in spite of recent hunter kills of about 1,200 cranes annually, representing about 6 percent of the total population. This number is slightly less than the annual estimated percentage of fledged juveniles in the population (8 percent), which would support a stable population model, assuming about 2 percent of the population dies annually through nonhunting causes.

References

Canterbury, J. L., P. A. Johnsgard, and H. F. Downing. 2013. *Birds and Birding in Wyoming's Bighorn Mountains Region*. Lincoln: Zea Books and University of Nebraska–Lincoln DigitalCommons. http://digitalcommons.unl.edu/zeabook/18/. 260 pp. Print edition available from http://www.lulu.com/shop/paul-a-johnsgard-and-jacqueline-l-canterbury-and-helen-f-downing/birds-and-birding-in-wyomings-bighorn-mountains-region/paperback/product-21777223.html.

Drewien, R. C., W. M. Brown, J. D. Varley, and D. C. Lockman. 1999. Seasonal movements of sandhill cranes radiomarked in Yellowstone National Park, Jackson Hole, Wyoming. *Journal of Wildlife Management* 63:126–136.

Johnsgard, P. A. 2012. Its crane season—in Wyoming. *Prairie Fire*, June 2012, pp. 1, 3, 4. http://www.prairiefirenewspaper.com/2012/06/its-crane-season-in-wyoming

Kruse, K. L., J. A. Dubovsky, and T. R. Cooper. 2013. *Status and Harvests of Sandhill Cranes: Mid-Continent, Rocky Mountain, Lower Colorado River Valley, and Eastern Populations*. Administrative Report, U.S. Fish and Wildlife Service, Lakewood, Colorado. 14 pp.

Kruse, K. L., D. E. Sharp, and J. A. Dubovsky. 2010. *Status and Harvests of Sandhill Cranes: Mid-Continent, Rocky Mountain, and Lower Colorado River Valley Populations*. Administrative Report, U.S. Fish and Wildlife Service, Denver, Colorado. 11 pp.

APPENDICES

Gray wolf

My Life in Biology

(Updated from the 2010 article in *Nebraska Bird Review* 78(3):103–126)

Childhood and Pre-College Years: 1931–1949

I was born June 28, 1931, in a very small town along the Red River in North Dakota, a town by the name of Christine, about twenty miles south of Fargo in southeast North Dakota, which at that time had barely a hundred residents, and probably about the same now. Christine was one of those little whistle-stop towns, and my earliest memories of nature are walking out along the railroad tracks gathering wildflowers for my mother. She encouraged my bringing back wildflowers for her, and watching local birds like red-winged blackbirds. In fact, when I started school, my first-grade teacher, Miss Evelyn Bilstead, had a mounted male red-winged blackbird in a glass Victorian bell jar, and knowing my interest in birds, she invited me to examine that beautiful bird up close. I can remember that as if it were yesterday, and that experience was an important aspect of my wanting to see live birds close. Sadly, Miss Bilstead died of a brain tumor only a few years later; several decades later I dedicated one of my bird books to her memory.

Christine is situated in the Red River valley, the bed of glacial Lake Agassiz. There was little natural habitat except along the wooded river. The railroad right-of-way had prairie grasses and other prairie plants, and also had native prairie birds like dickcissels, meadowlarks, and the like. However, I had no knowledge of any bird identification guides.

My mother grew up on a farm about fifteen miles west of Christine, in Barrie Township. My great-grandparents (Charles and Ada

Morgan) had moved there in 1876. The Morgan farm is located near the present-day Sheyenne National Grassland, the only significant area of tallgrass prairie remaining in North Dakota. It was through my mother's help and books that I first saw and learned to identify native prairie plants and came to love such breeding birds as marbled godwits and bobolinks.

In 1939 we moved twenty miles south to Wahpeton, North Dakota. Wahpeton had a far better and bigger school, extending through high school, than Christine's four-room school that encompassed only the elementary grades. Wahpeton's public library was one of its critically important features for me. I can visualize to this day exactly where the bird books were, and what was there. In fact, a couple of years ago I went back and saw with pleasure that they still had the copy of Roberts's two-volume *Birds of Minnesota* that used to give me so much pleasure.

I spent a lot of time in the Wahpeton library, and in drawing birds. I read books on natural history as well as all kinds of popular subjects, such as adventure stories, but especially books about animals. I was also active in building model airplanes, collecting rocks, and observing wild plants.

Mother encouraged all of my activities. Her sister Beatrice lived in Detroit, Michigan, and at least by our standards seemed very wealthy. After she realized I was so interested in birds, she would send me wonderful bird books for Christmas. My still-treasured and well-worn copy of Audubon's *The Birds of America* came from her in 1939.

Waterfowl became increasingly of interest to me through my mother's cousin, H. R. "Bud" Morgan. When I was about eleven years old, Bud started taking me along on his spring duck counts and helped me to identify waterfowl. At that time he was a state game warden, but he eventually became director of the North Dakota Game and Parks Commission. In memory of his love of nature and his conservation work, a forty-acre tract of woodlands and sandhills along the Sheyenne River was designated the H. R. Morgan State Nature Preserve.

In 1943, when I was thirteen, my parents gave me a copy of F. H. Kortright's *Ducks, Geese, and Swans of North America* for Christmas. I practically memorized it and dreamed that one day I might know enough about waterfowl to write a similar book (which I finally did thirty-two years later).

In high school I was active in choir and acting in class plays. I wasn't compulsive about grades in high school and had only an adequate grade point average, but it was good enough to get into the National Honor Society. Athletics were of no interest. With an eye to eventually writing for publication, I took a class in journalism and wrote for the high school yearbook. I also enrolled in typing, which required special permission from the principal because at that time only girls were permitted to take typing. The biology course I took was taught by the school basketball coach, who knew virtually nothing about it. For graduation and at my request my parents gave me a pair of 6×20 binoculars (and a small suitcase), both of which served me well for about six years.

Undergraduate College: 1949–1953

I attended the North Dakota State School of Science in Wahpeton from 1949 to 1951. That is a two-year college with a trade school and a liberal arts program, so I received a junior college diploma in liberal arts. The biology course I took there was regrettably taught by the same man who taught my high school biology class, as in the interim he had become the basketball coach there! I essentially slept through the course and took some pleasure in acting as if I actually were asleep, waiting for the teacher to suddenly call on me to answer what he thought would stump me. After a few such tricks he stopped calling on me. I completed the course with the highest average in the class. Almost fifty years later, when I was home for a funeral, the instructor saw me on the streets of Wahpeton and proudly told me that I had been his all-time favorite student!

The most useful classes I took at North Dakota were German

(knowing I would someday need to learn it to pass a graduate-school foreign language exam) and English literature. I loved reading Shakespeare, and after taking an exam on *Hamlet*, I received such a high score that the professor called me aside, saying that he had never before given such a high score and asking me how I had managed to so effectively cheat on it!

Only two choices were available for me then as to further education. One was North Dakota State University (then called North Dakota Agricultural College) in Fargo, and the other was the University of North Dakota at Grand Forks, with an undergraduate program that was strongly oriented toward medicine. But Fargo had a program in zoology, and I could get a bachelor's degree in biology, with a major in zoology.

When I transferred to North Dakota Agricultural College as a junior, I was still thinking of a career in wildlife. My advisor there, J. Frank Cassel, had graduated from Cornell University and had recently finished a PhD from Colorado State University. During registration I told Dr. Cassel that I already had a detailed plan for graduation, with every course listed that I wanted to take in the next two years. He said he had never before seen a student show up prepared like that, knowing exactly what he wanted and needed to take over the next six quarters. He soon started orienting me toward studying ornithology, which I hadn't known to be a possible profession. I completed majors in both zoology and in botany, and became quite interested in plant ecology, mostly because of a great teacher named Loren Potter.

During that time I became more highly concerned about doing well academically, at least in science, and maintained a straight A average in both zoology and botany. While a junior at North Dakota State, Dr. Cassel encouraged me to apply for a small (twenty-five dollars) scholarship that was given every year to some student who wanted to do a special research project over the summer between his or her junior and senior year. Dr. Cassel encouraged me to do a bibliographic survey of the waterfowl of North Dakota. I would try to summarize in a card file what was available in published and unpublished information sources on the distribution of North Dakota waterfowl.

I received the scholarship and soon decided that as long as I was assembling the waterfowl data, I might as well include all the other North Dakota birds too. North Dakota didn't then (and still doesn't) have a state bird book, or even a well-documented modern summary of its avifauna. I scanned the local libraries and drove to several of the state's national wildlife refuges, where I extracted large amounts of information on North Dakota's birds. My collection became a very large card file. I also wrote a typescript summary, consisting of an annotated list of all the species of North Dakota birds for which I could find any data. So far as I know, nothing was ever done with it.

I received the twenty-five dollars (and also a bonus copy of Bent's *Life Histories of North American Gallinaceous Birds*) for that work. More importantly, Dr. Cassel suggested that I use the waterfowl data to write a booklet on the waterfowl of North Dakota, which he said he could probably arrange to have published. After I had finished the text, he asked me to also do some drawings for it. I did four sheets of pen-and-ink drawings, showing all North Dakota's common waterfowl, plus some other similar water birds, such as grebes. I made the drawings in a manner similar to those in the early Peterson field guides and wrote to Roger Peterson to ask if I could use his idea of using arrows to point out important field marks. (Recently I learned from the curator at the Roger Tory Peterson Institute of Natural History that they still have correspondence from me dating back to the 1950s, filed under "Correspondence with famous people"!) That sixteen-page booklet was published through a consortium of three local colleges (Concordia, Moorhead State, and North Dakota State) called the Institute of Regional Studies.

That project gave me some confidence that I could write, and that furthermore I could draw well enough for publication. I'd never had any training in writing or art, and never had any English courses beyond freshman English composition. The experience probably gave me more confidence about writing than was warranted.

Washington State College: 1953–1956

When I asked him for advice on graduate schools, Dr. Cassel told me I could become an ornithologist rather than working for a game commission, teaching ornithology, or working for one of the environmental organizations then in existence. I applied to graduate programs in Pullman, Washington; Corvallis, Oregon; and Logan, Utah, all of which had strong programs in waterfowl biology. I was admitted to all of them. I chose Washington State College (now Washington State University) for two reasons. My older brother was already there in a PhD program. More importantly, Professor Charles Yocom had recently written a book called *Waterfowl and Their Food Plants in Washington*, and he strongly encouraged me to come and study waterfowl ecology under him.

Regrettably, Dr. Yocom accepted a post at Humboldt State College about a week or two after I arrived at Pullman, so I was left without an advisor for waterfowl research. Furthermore, Dr. Yocom had agreed that I could undertake a master's degree program in waterfowl ecology, with a degree in zoology, not wildlife management. That had been an oral commitment on his part, on which the department later reneged. Instead, the Zoology Department chairman insisted that my degree had to be in wildlife management rather than zoology because of the source of my funding.

The botany department's ecologist was Professor Rexford Daubenmire, who was the most inspiring of all the teachers I encountered at Washington State. I took all of his courses, and he served with Dr. George Hudson (mammalogist and curator of the college museum) and Dr. I. O. Buss (gallinaceous gamebird biologist) as my graduate committee. The well-known avian physiologist Dr. Donald Farner was also there, and I worked as an assistant for him one summer, caring for sparrows and recording bird activity data related to migration energy expenditure. James King was then still a graduate student of Farner's, and Jared Verner, Alan Wilson, and Frank Golley were also graduate student friends who later became a nationally known ornithologist, evolutionary biologist, and mammalogist, respectively.

For my MS research, I did an ecological study on a sand dune region in central Washington called the Potholes. It was then an area much like Nebraska's Sandhills, with a high water table and many marshes and wet meadows at the base of the dunes. A large dam (O'Sullivan Dam) had recently been built that was inundating many of those wetlands. I was there to try to determine how the changes in water levels were affecting biological populations, especially waterfowl. For my thesis I did a general ecological study of the plants and water birds relative to these water fluctuations. I lived in an old Bureau of Land Management house, which had been occupied while O'Sullivan Dam was being constructed, and traveled by ten-foot wooden boat and outboard motor to my study sites across the still-expanding reservoir.

While I was at Washington State, I became aware of the Wildfowl Trust in England. Peter Scott (later Sir Peter Scott), a famous waterfowl artist, had developed the trust after World War II as a place for collecting, breeding, and conserving as many of the species of the world's waterfowl as possible. I wrote to Scott, saying that when I finished graduate school, I would like to come to the Wildfowl Trust and study the comparative behavior of the world's waterfowl. He wrote back to the effect that if I could find a way of financial support, they would be happy to let me do such research there. That was a dream that I kept in my heart for the better part of six years.

My main research study was published in the journal *Ecology*, but while doing fieldwork I also worked on many minor projects. For example, I obtained data on duck sex ratios, which I later published in the *Journal of Wildlife Management*. I was also fascinated by waterfowl courtship activity and spent many hours watching ducks courting and making field sketches. As far as I could tell, some of my observations were new, so I submitted and published them in the Cooper Society's journal *The Condor*. I later received a letter from Professor Charles Sibley of Cornell University who wrote that, although it was an interesting paper, I obviously was not aware of the work of Dr. Konrad Lorenz, who had published a very extensive paper in a German journal on courtship behavior in the dabbling ducks. This news was highly embarrassing, but Dr. Sibley also asked if I would be interested in coming to Cornell for a PhD. I had thought about Cornell University ever since my days at North Dakota State, when Dr. Cassel had strongly recommended I try to go to Cornell for a graduate degree. In fact, I had almost applied to Cornell graduate school, but I didn't think I would be accepted, and it furthermore cost twenty-five dollars just to apply.

I finished my master's degree at Washington in 1955 but stayed a second year partly so I could marry Lois Lampe, who in 1956 finished her MS in plant ecology under Professor Daubenmire. Although I had also been accepted to study under Professor Alden Miller at the University of California as a graduate teaching assistant, I did decide to go to Cornell. With Dr. Sibley's support, I was accepted to the then Conservation Department's PhD program and also awarded the best graduate fellowship that Cornell offered.

Lois and I were married in June 1956, and after buying an ancient Ford four-door sedan for twenty-five dollars and a two-wheel trailer for thirty dollars, we left for Ithaca with less than one hundred dollars in my pockets. The car had no functional first gear, so a few steep hills in Dubuque, Iowa, had to be ascended in reverse. Miraculously, the car had gotten us to within about ten miles from Ithaca, when a state patrol officer stopped us for lacking a valid New York trailer license. We had to unload the trailer and leave all its contents in the ditch before going on to Ithaca. I returned the next day and, in a few trips, got our remaining possessions to Ithaca. Remarkably, none of the trailer's contents had been stolen (not surprisingly, because they had little actual value). For my driving infraction I was fined a minimal ten dollars by a kindly Trumansburg judge, who told me I legally should have been allowed thirty days in which to obtain a New York trailer license. The car lasted another year; I quickly gave the trailer away rather than get it licensed.

Cornell University: 1956–1959

Choosing Cornell was a decision that affected the rest of my life. I was thinking by 1956 that I would become a teacher or researcher rather than a wildlife biologist. Dr. Sibley encouraged me to work on waterfowl behavior for my PhD research. He was then interested in waterfowl as examples of the results of selection against hybridization and their associated behavioral isolating mechanisms. I spent three years at Cornell (1956–59) working on the evolutionary relationships of North American mallard-like ducks, including the mallards, American black duck, Mexican duck, mottled duck, and Florida duck. I studied their comparative pair-forming behavior and comparative morphology, as well as doing some protein electrophoresis of blood serum, trying to estimate their relationships and evolutionary history.

Dr. Sibley proved to be the most intellectually stimulating teacher I have ever known. He was also one of the most demanding and, at times, tyrannical. His famous temper made all of his students quake in his presence and regard him as a godlike figure to be disobeyed only at one's utter peril. Yet he could also be charmingly funny, and also endlessly interesting. He attracted overflow crowds to his introductory ornithology classes, captivating them with his great lecturing ability and complete command of his subject.

My three years at Cornell were spent on full fellowship, so I never had to act as one of Dr. Sibley's often suffering graduate assistants; however, I did work for him as a lab technician during the summer of 1958. That summer was a critical one in Dr. Sibley's transformation from species-level taxonomy using whole-specimen data to a much more molecular taxonomic approach. He had obtained a one-year National Science Foundation (NSF) grant for a pilot study on the feasibility of evaluating avian blood proteins as a taxonomic tool, using paper electrophoresis. He assigned me the job of running the electrophoretic separations, as well as obtaining a variety of domestic birds from the poultry department and various game birds from the state-operated game farm near Ithaca. I shuttled these birds back and forth, obtaining blood samples and running their serum analyses.

These efforts, unfortunately, produced extremely disheartening results, owing to great individual variability in the serum profiles. Nevertheless, Dr. Sibley and I coauthored two papers on our blood studies.

While reviewing the waterfowl literature, I encountered a paper written by Robert McCabe and H. F. Deutsch, which had been published in the *Wilson Bulletin* about a decade previously. Their study indicated that significant interspecies differences exist in the electrophoretic profiles of egg-white proteins from various game birds. I decided to confirm and extend their findings, using eggs that the birds happened to lay while in our aviary, or that I otherwise obtained from the Poultry Science Department. I had to do this experiment surreptitiously because I would be dealt with harshly should Dr. Sibley discover my departure from his strict protocol. Near summer's end, Dr. Sibley proclaimed our efforts on blood protein to be a failure and announced that he would not ask for more NSF money to continue the study. Gathering my courage, I then fearfully showed him the results from the egg-white samples I had analyzed. Within minutes he grasped their taxonomic potential and immediately laid plans for a new grant to undertake a massive electrophoretic survey of North American birds.

Soon after that I began to feel like the sorcerer's apprentice, for that event marked the start of his wholesale egg-collecting activities, first in the United States and later worldwide. He was quite relentless in this, and eventually had serious legal trouble for using egg whites from some federally endangered species, such as the peregrine. However, his work was among the first to exploit molecular biology for higher-level taxonomy of the world's birds. This led directly to his later research using DNA-DNA hybridization, which shook the avian taxonomic tree to its very roots.

At Cornell I became fully exposed to Professor Sibley's interests in evolution, taxonomy, comparative behavior, and pure ornithology. Additionally, Professor Lamont Cole, a famous animal population ecologist; Professor Ari van Tienhoven, a poultry science professor; and Dr. Bill Dilger, an ethologist working on thrushes and parrots composed my committee. All of them were important to me. I also met Professor Ernst Mayr while I was there. He was already a biological icon, but I evidently impressed him enough so that when the second edition of James Peters's *Check-list of Birds of the World* was being planned, he asked me to revise the waterfowl and screamer families (*Anseriformes*) for the first volume of that edition.

During my final year at Cornell, I approached Dr. Sibley and said that I wanted to try to get a post-doctoral grant and spend a year in England studying comparative waterfowl behavior at the Wildfowl Trust. Dr. Sibley suggested that, instead, he could apply for a research grant as the prime investigator, and I could be his assistant. I immediately rejected that approach and applied for two post-doctoral fellowships, one from the NSF and the other from the U.S. Public Health Service, hoping that with great good fortune I might get one. Luckily, I got both of them! I was thus able to spend two years at the trust, one after the other, which was the single most important event of my life because that gave me two years to do what I had most wanted to do for many years.

The Wildfowl Trust, England: 1959–1961

The Wildfowl Trust (now the Wildlife and Wetlands Trust) is in part a zoo, getting much of its income from people coming to see the birds, but it is also a major research organization. At the time I was there (1959–61), it was at the peak of its development, having what was the largest collection, both in species and numbers of waterfowl, that had ever been assembled. Peter Scott was internationally famous (he was later knighted) and was actively bringing back rare birds from everywhere in the world. They then had about 120 of the 145 living species of ducks, geese, and swans, or more than 80 percent of the entire family Anatidae. So I was lucky to get there just when the trust was at its very best, with the highest number of species in its history.

The trust had a resident staff that was mostly concerned with avicultural problems, such as nutrition or disease. Most of the staff was

113

doing applied research, relative to either the waterfowl collection or to the conservation of waterfowl in Great Britain. However, Dr. G. V. T. Mathews was there as science director, and Dr. Janet Kear arrived my second year, as assistant director of research. Hugh Boyd was their waterfowl expert.

Only a few weeks after I arrived at the trust in the summer of 1959, an Ethological Congress was held at Oxford University. I went over on the first day by bus, arriving late in the afternoon. After registering, I was directed to the hall where everybody was already gathered for the dinner meal. The hall was quite crowded but at its far end I could see Dr. Sibley, sitting at a large table slightly elevated from the rest. With him were such personal idols as Konrad Lorenz and Niko Tinbergen, plus a few other people I didn't recognize. There was an empty seat right beside Dr. Sibley, so I walked up and sat down beside him. He stared at me incredulously and informed me that I had sat down at High Table, and one must be invited to sit there. I was greatly embarrassed and quickly got up to leave, when the others laughed and motioned for me to sit. As a result of my naiveté I was able to get to know Lorenz, the author of the duck behavior paper I had overlooked, and Professor Tinbergen, already famous for his work on gull and fish behavior. Both shared the Nobel Prize in 1972, and Lorenz also wrote a letter endorsing me for the Guggenheim Fellowship that I received in the 1970s.

I was able to study pure comparative behavioral research and its taxonomic implications full time while at the trust. Within a year I had about six papers in press, was well into the writing of one book, and had started a second. The first book was an attempt to summarize all the observations I made on the behavior of the birds there, toward developing a world survey of comparative waterfowl behavior. That effort became the *Handbook of Waterfowl Behavior* and was the first comparative behavioral survey of any family of birds. Second, I also began to write a book that was directed to the general public, trying to describe what I thought was most interesting about waterfowl.

By then Lois and I had one child, Jay, and our second, Scott, was born there during our first year in England. Scott was named after Peter Scott (later Sir Peter Scott). He was not only a great painter but also a national hero for his exploits during World War II. He also was a great hero for me because of how much he had influenced my life's work.

In any case, the main goal for my time at the trust was writing my comparative behavior book on the waterfowl family Anatidae. That was going to be my major contribution to ornithology. It was almost ready to be submitted when I left England in 1961, but I held off submitting it in hopes of getting some information on a few more little-known species. I submitted it to Cornell University Press in 1964, and it was published in 1965. It eventually went through two printings.

University of Nebraska: 1961–2015

From the autumn of 1959 until the summer of 1961 I was busily engaged in postdoctoral fellowship research at the Wildfowl Trust. The trust was a grand place for doing research but a very poor one from which to look for jobs in America. One day in the spring of 1961, I received a letter from Dr. Sibley which said that he had just learned from his Nebraska contacts that there was teaching job in ornithology open at the University of Nebraska. He had spent several summers in the Platte River valley during the 1950s, collecting hundreds of birds, mainly various hybridizing species-pairs such as flickers, buntings, orioles, and grosbeaks. With a hint of Ivy League superiority, he added, "Nebraska would not be a bad place from which to look for another job."

I didn't know anything about the University of Nebraska, or even much about the state. However, I remembered that H. A. (Al) Hochbaum, who was the director of Delta Research Station at Delta Marsh, Manitoba, had told me that in his opinion Nebraska was second only to North Dakota for prime wetland habitat and duck production. I thus thought that Nebraska might be a good place to study waterfowl ecology.

I applied for and was soon offered the job as an instructor—sight unseen, without even a phone interview. So I arrived in late summer without ever having seen the campus, Lincoln, or the state. We moved to Lincoln in August 1961, about the time our daughter Ann was born. I was to teach general zoology, my major responsibility, and to develop a course in ornithology, plus any others I might want to devise. Dr. Harold Manter, the Zoology Department chair, later told me that, because I was applying from abroad, it was thought that I would probably accept the job as an instructor, rather than an assistant professor. However, I was not only promoted to assistant professor at the end of my first year but more importantly received tenure at that time. To my knowledge I have been the only person at the University of Nebraska ever to advance from instructor to assistant professor with tenure at the end of his first year.

Our department was known as the Zoology Department at that time. Dr. Manter was a national figure, known for his parasitology work. Including him, the department then consisted of about seven people. We later merged with the three-person Botany Department to form a Department of Life Sciences, and still later became a separate School of Biological Sciences.

My first graduate student, Roger Sharpe, arrived for the fall semester of 1961 and started work on a master's degree, studying the courtship behavior of some captive-raised mallard × northern pintail hybrids. He was an avid birder and knew many good birding places in Nebraska. It was he who first told me about the sandhill cranes of the Platte valley. When I took my ornithology class there the following March, not many cranes were near Grand Island, so we drove on to Elm Creek before turning south off highway 34 and crossing the Platte River bridge. I was soon astounded by the sight of thousands of cranes in the meadows along the river. After that initial 1962 trip, I became intensely interested in sandhill cranes and the Platte valley. My first book on cranes was published in 1981—*Those of the Gray Wind*—and in 1983 *Cranes of the World* appeared. My first book on the Platte valley, *Channels in Time*, appeared in 1984, and *Crane*

Music was published in 1991. Other books on cranes and the Platte valley followed.

Roger Sharpe also knew of a prairie chicken lek at Burchard Lake Wildlife Management Area, about eighty miles southeast of Lincoln, so I regularly took my ornithology classes there. Sharpe eventually worked on the comparative behavior of prairie-chickens (greater, lesser, and Attwater's) for his PhD research. Grouse studies soon also became very important to me. My first book on grouse—*Grouse and Quails of North America*—appeared in 1973. The second, *Grouse of the World*, followed in 1981, and *Grassland Grouse and Their Conservation* appeared in 2001.

I fell in love with Nebraska from the very beginning. I very soon decided I wanted to stay at the University of Nebraska forever. With the help of NSF grants I made many extended field trips. After a brief trip in 1961 to help capture and band molting Steller's eiders, I went to Alaska again in 1963 and worked on spectacled eider behavior. I went to Australia in 1964 to observe some aberrant Australian ducks, such as the musk duck and freckled duck. Our daughter Karin was born while I was out of touch in the Murray River Valley. I went to the Andes of South America in 1965, studying as many populations of the Andean torrent duck as possible, trying to determine how many species or subspecies of that highly variable duck should be recognized.

When I started working on grouse and quails in the 1970s, I traveled to southern Mexico and Yucatan on another NSF grant to study the ecology and vocalizations of some of the rare New World quail species. This work greatly aided the preparation for my writing of *Grouse and Quails of North America*. I also later studied the courtship and territoriality of rock ptarmigan in Newfoundland, and of black grouse and capercaillies in Scotland, while preparing my *Grouse of the World* on a Guggenheim fellowship.

A long series of world or continental monographs on bird groups followed, such as on shorebirds, pheasants, quails, raptors, hummingbirds, trogons, pelecaniform birds, and others. And there were some books on subjects such as diving birds (*Diving Birds of North America*), desert-adapted birds (*Birds of Dry Places*), the avian social parasites (*Deception at the Nest*), as well as lek-forming birds and associated aspects of sexual selection (*Arena Birds*).

Over the years, I also increasingly became more interested in the biological diversity of Nebraska and the Great Plains. I began studies that led to books on the biodiversity and ecology of the state (*The Nature of Nebraska*), the Sandhills (*This Fragile Land*), the Platte River (*Channels in Time*), and the Niobrara River (*A River Running through Time*). The Great Plains also served as a subject for several books (*Birds of the Great Plains, Great Wildlife of the Great Plains, Faces of the Great Plains*), as did Great Plains history (*Lewis and Clark on the Great Plains, Wind through the Buffalo Grass*). Interests in the grassland ecosystems of the Great Plains led me to write both *Prairie Birds* and *Prairie Dog Empire*.

Scholarly Activities

Technical and Popular Writing

During the 1960s we had a small faculty club at the university, which was just an opportunity to have lunch in an old sorority house. Many faculty members went there to eat lunch. So I often ate there, and one of the people whom I enjoyed sitting with was Bruce Nicoll, who was director of the University of Nebraska Press. He had been with the university for a long time, and would tell us all sorts of fascinating things about its history. I would just sit there and listen, never contributing much to the conversation.

One day in late 1965, shortly after my *Handbook of Waterfowl Behavior* was published, I was eating quietly at the club. Suddenly Bruce Nicoll stormed in, waving a copy of the *New York Times* in his hand and saying, "God dammit, Johnsgard, what's the big idea?" When I said I didn't know what he was talking about, he showed me a favorable review of my book in the newspaper's book review section. He soon calmed down and asked me what book I was currently writing.

I replied that I had an essentially finished book manuscript in my office files but doubted that it was publishable. Nevertheless, he followed me back to my office, where I dug out the manuscript from my files.

Bruce took the manuscript with him, and only a day later called back to say he wanted to publish it! I had doubts about the book's saleability but thought that some color plates might help. He replied that I could include up to two sixteen-page signatures of color plates. *Waterfowl: Their Biology and Natural History* was published in 1968. Almost immediately it won a design award from the Chicago Book Clinic and was also chosen by the Federation of the English Speaking Peoples to be one of the books they place in their libraries around the world. It was also named one of the hundred best science books of the year. After that book's success, I began to think I could write popular nature books that included a good deal of information on natural history.

Another of the unexpected circumstances that affected my life occurred in 1972. One day while signing some copies of *Waterfowl: Their Biology and Natural History* at a local bookstore, I learned that John Neihardt had also recently signed some copies of *Black Elk Speaks*. I bought a copy and read it that afternoon. I think of all the books I have read, I was never so mesmerized as by that one. I stayed awake for hours that evening, wondering how I could respond in some real way to that book, in which snow geese appeared during several of Black Elk's visions.

I had already been thinking about doing a book on the snow goose and wondered if I could somehow counterpoint what I knew about the biology of snow geese with the Native American view of snow geese. Finally, in the early morning hours I decided that I couldn't sleep, so I might just as well get up and start writing. I wrote more or less secretively for about five weeks or so. By then the writing was almost done, except for a section dealing with the arctic breeding grounds, which I hadn't previously visited.

When the manuscript was essentially done, I thought I'd better have somebody read it critically. I gave it to Vicki Peterson, one of our departmental secretaries who had done some manuscript retyping for me, and asked her if she would read it. She brought it back the next day and told me she thought it was by far the best writing I had ever done. I then decided I would send it to three publishers. Two of them rejected it fairly rapidly, but Doubleday indicated that it was very interested. I replied that I would need a few more months to write the remaining part, so I could visit the snow goose's tundra breeding grounds, but I would have it done by fall.

In early June of 1973 I went to Churchill, Manitoba, with the aid of a small American Philosophical Society grant. From Churchill I was able to visit a large snow goose nesting colony at La Perouse Bay, courtesy of Professor Fred Cooke, who was researching the colony. While at Churchill I met Robert Montgomerie, who showed me some of his friend Paul Geraghty's ink drawings. I thought they were the kind of mystical images that I wanted to use to somehow capture the mysticism of the geese in Neihardt's book. So I wrote to Geraghty, sending him a copy of my manuscript, and asked him if he would be interested in illustrating it. He replied that it was exactly the sort of thing he would love to illustrate. I think his illustrations were a critically important part of that book's success. Native American legends and myths are also an important aspect of that book, included mostly because my ancestry is in small part Native American.

After my snow goose book appeared in 1974, I decided that I could write popular but accurate books, which not only increased my annual income but also increased my confidence and personal pleasure in my writing, With the success of my snow goose book, my writing life took a somewhat new direction. I decided to write a combination of professionally directed technical books, toward a fairly restricted ornithological audience, but also to spend just as much time writing for a much broader audience, on natural history, environmental, and conservation topics.

The ultimate in my popular writing was a dragon and unicorn book, *Dragons and Unicorns: A Natural History*, which I wrote with our daughter Karin when she was in high school. I thought that if I was ever going to be fired for writing something frivolous, it would probably be for that. The book was mostly a whimsical metaphor on conservation ethics, with some political and religious satire thrown in. It has sold more copies than any other of my titles and has since remained in press continuously.

Writing Influences

I have often been asked how and why I am such a prolific writer. Annie Dillard wrote in *The Writing Life* that there are maybe twenty people on the planet who can produce an average of one book per year, and she thought that number was probably about the maximum possible for anyone. During the fifty years between my first book in 1965 and 2015, I have published nearly seventy hardbound books and about ten electronic-only book-length publications.

I confess that my writing is a total compulsion. There is another rationalization for my writing, and I've thought about it often. There is hardly anybody else I know of who writes well, draws adequately, and photographs reasonably well, and who can by himself put together a book on some major subject. I'm one of the very few, maybe the only one I know of, who can do all those things adequately. When growing up I thought it would be a wonderful thing to have a book about loons, for example, or a book about pheasants. By and large, they weren't then available, so I have made a serious effort to produce them.

Al Hochbaum, whom I mentioned earlier, once talked to me about writing. At that time he had written *Canvasback on a Prairie Marsh* and *Travels and Traditions of Waterfowl*. He said he planned on doing seven drafts of his manuscript before it was ready for publication. When I told him I write one draft, retype it myself or have a secretary retype it, and then consider it ready to submit, I don't think he believed me.

I've also never outlined a book, a chapter, or any other writing project. My older brother, Keith, once wrote a book on the psychological values of exercise and told me that he prepared a seventy-page prospectus for the book before he found a publisher. I told him that I normally don't contact a publisher until the manuscript is complete. Instead I typically write a one-page letter, asking if they would like to consider it for publication.

When writing a reference book on birds, or any of my geographically oriented books, I feel I can write in short blocks of time, with a fair number of disturbances, without affecting the flow of writing. When I'm trying to write a chapter in something like the snow goose book I'm bothered greatly by interference. I need to have a sort of stable mental state to write well. In fact, if I'm worried about something, I'm terrible at creative writing. For example, on a Saturday or Sunday, there is usually no disturbance on campus. Then I can count on having many hours without even the phone ringing.

I usually came to campus every Saturday to write, except on football game days. One year I paid more than $120 in fines for parking on campus during football Saturdays. I finally decided that was too expensive and I had to give it up, especially after my car was towed away one day. That was one of the many reasons I came to hate football, the Husker/Big Red mania, and the coddling of football players, who soon learned to avoid all my classes. Because of my no-nonsense attitude toward football, Bob Devaney dictated (in a letter to me, copied to the university's president) that I would thereafter be denied for life the privilege of buying football tickets at Memorial Stadium. I considered it a badge of honor.

I write three general kinds of books. First is the overall topic of specific birds or bird groups, which represents most of my titles. Second, I like to write about biologically interesting places, such as the Platte, Tetons, Nebraska Sandhills, and Niobrara River. Last, there are more general topics, such the book I wrote with my daughter Karin on the mythology of dragons and unicorns, the biology and ecology of social parasitism in birds such as the Old World cuckoos, and the biology and history of the Lewis and Clark expedition.

My usual procedure, after deciding to write a book on a bird group, was often to get out a field guide and flip through its pages to try to decide what group hasn't already been covered well. Then, as soon as I picked a group, I would go back to the *Zoological Record, Biological Abstracts*, and every other bibliographic source I could think of and start filling out five-by-seven-inch reference cards, often until I had about a thousand.

Once I started writing, I could generally produce anywhere from two thousand to five thousand words per day. I would do about four to five hours of actual writing in a good day. For example, I might write for two and a half hours in the morning, then take a break and do something else, and then write two or three hours in the afternoon. I think my primary skill, especially in writing bird books for the general public, has been in assimilating lots of information and putting it in an understandable form.

I prepared dozens of card files, covering topics for each active book prior to putting all my references into computer files. I usually put together a minimum of about five hundred references, up to a maximum of about two thousand. Then, once I had the references assembled, I would go back to the literature and begin photocopying the appropriate parts of those references. I then began building separate files of photocopied materials relating to a species or chapter. Virtually all of the research money I received at the university went for photocopying.

My next step varies some, but I try to read over all the material that I have in a file, and then start writing. Then it's a combination of writing and going back to either the photocopies, or to the library to pull out some other source. Normally my writing was interrupted by classes at least once a day. I typically had a midmorning class, so I would write until that class, and then I would be done until the lunch hour. I would start again in the afternoon, depending on my class schedule.

I enjoy both factual and creative writing. I enjoy the creative writing simply because it's creative. I enjoy the other because I'm fairly good at it. I like to think at the end of a day I have extracted the important stuff about this topic in a clear and interesting way. And it's rewarding to think that, if I can compress all the important information on a complex topic down to about three hundred to five hundred readable manuscript pages, I've achieved something useful.

One late-winter day in the late 1990s, while I was in my office writing, I had a phone call. When I answered it, a woman at the other end of the line simply asked, "Are you the big bird honcho of Nebraska?" When I tentatively answered in the affirmative, she identified herself as Jo D Blessing, and further said, "I teach fourth grade in Elwood Public School, and I need some field guides to teach my kids about bird identification." She then said that if I would provide her some field guides, she would make me a gooseberry pie. I had never eaten gooseberry pie, but it seemed to be too good an offer to turn down. I told her that I could probably provide about four or five and would soon be traveling to Kearney for an Audubon birding festival, where we could make the trade.

We found each other without difficulty in the Kearney Holiday Inn—she was the only person carrying a pie, and I was wearing a red baseball cap slightly edited to read "No Big Red"). After making the trade, Jo D coaxed me into going to Elwood to talk about birds to her students. While I was at Elwood, she showed me her classroom's pitifully small library (mainly an old set of the *World Book Encyclopedia*), which reminded me of the paltry assortment of books that had been in Christine's primary school. On my long drive home, I vowed that I would write a book on the natural history of Nebraska that might be of value to teachers, students, and the general public. The book appeared in 2001—*The Nature of Nebraska*—and was dedicated to "the children of Nebraska, and especially the fourth grade class at Elwood Public School."

Until about 1977, I continued writing books on the old manual Underwood typewriter that the Zoology Department had provided me, when a secretary friend convinced me I should invest in an IBM Selectric typewriter. I then wrote several books with that wonderful machine, but in the early 1980s our kids started telling me about the values of computers for writing. However, it wasn't until I had my 1984 heart attack that I began using a computer. Scott and Karin had convinced me that I should buy a computer and learn how to compose text on it. I thus bought two Apple IIe desktop computers in the early 1980s, thinking at least the kids would be able to use them. By serendipity, one was in my bedroom when I got home from my 1984 heart attack, ready for me to learn how to use it.

I now keep three computers on twenty-four hours a day, using one for text writing, another for Internet and email use, and a third for storing and editing photos. By using computers I have almost always kept several (and rarely up to seven or eight) book projects going simultaneously. That is possible because the manuscripts are invariably at different stages, and there is always something that can be worked on at the moment.

Typically, publishing a book with a commercial press has taken me at least one year. However, because of the mechanics of academic book publishing, with two or three reviewers and other time delays, it's more often closer to two or three years for university press books.

Reading and Literary Influences

As to favorite authors, I have read Aldo Leopold far more than Henry David Thoreau. I received Leopold's *A Sand County Almanac* for Christmas in 1949, when I was eighteen. My parents gave it to me shortly after it had appeared, when it was in its second printing. It became a kind of bible, in the sense of representing a special writing style for me, and something that I wanted to emulate.

Aldo Leopold has always been my ideal as a person who wrote superbly about nature. I admire his use of wild animals and natural events as the source of parables, and his ability to see greater lessons in small events. He could tell a simple story, like cutting down an oak tree, for example, and describe the history of Wisconsin as represented by the rings of the oak. Much the same thing appeals to me in Annie Dillard's writing. She could see a frog in a pond, or a shed snakeskin, and somehow enlarge that into a near-cosmic event, something far greater than just one's simple nature observations.

125

I especially admire Aldo Leopold for being able to write both cleanly and poetically, and Annie Dillard for being able to see and describe simple events as having a completely different and broader significance. I've often thought that if I could write as well as Aldo Leopold did, it would be a wonderful gift, but I knew I would never be able to write like Annie Dillard. I corresponded with her for a time, after two of our books (*Song of the North Wind* and *Pilgrim at Tinker Creek*) were reviewed in the same column of a New York newspaper. She even let me critique a story she was writing for *Harper's* about her trip to the Galapagos Islands.

Time magazine also was a model for clear writing for me while in college. I thought that *Time's* writing style, which was very clear and precise, was what I should try to emulate. I often would read *Time* with the idea of analyzing how their writers managed to summarize information and ideas.

At times I have been purposefully anthropomorphic in my writing, even though in my animal behavior class I would rail against anthropomorphism. I don't use it in technical writing reference books, but I do use it fairly often in popular writing. Aldo Leopold was rather anthropomorphic in some of his writing, so I felt that if he could do it, so can I. I do so knowingly, as in talking about rivers in a sort of anthropomorphic way, certain that people know that it is simply poetic license. My snow goose book was certainly anthropomorphic. After some thought, I gave Inuit names to the geese I described to help readers remember and identify with them.

I must confess that the longer I live and the more I watch birds, the more I believe that maybe a little bit of anthropomorphism is warranted. I'm absolutely convinced that there is a lot more to what they know and perceive, as compared to an individual human's capacity to interpret them. I honestly think that we are underestimating birds, and certainly other mammals, when we avoid anthropomorphism rigorously.

Drawing and Wood Sculpture

Essentially all my artwork for publication has been done in pen and ink. By the time I got to graduate school, we were told we had to do everything for publication in Rapidograph lettering with Rapidograph technical pens using India ink. The first drawings I did—even the undergraduate booklet that I did on waterfowl of North Dakota—was done in India ink with a technical pen. I used that technique for quite a number of years simply because I was under the assumption that that was what was needed for reproduction.

Then, maybe by chance, I realized I could start using other black non-India ink, and especially nylon-tipped pens with very fine points, as they became available. I could get fairly dark, if not black, colors that were acceptable to publishers. So I went to that technique, as it was less messy, and I could get graded widths and intensities of line. I also learned how to use scratchboard. The drawings in *Waterfowl: Their Biology and Natural History* were nearly all scratchboard drawings. I used that approach for only that one book, as it was far too time consuming. Most of the hundreds of drawings in my *Handbook of Waterfowl Behavior* were made from 16mm movie film, by taking individual frames and enlarging them. I then made ink drawings based on those enlargements, so they weren't based on less accurate field sketches.

My wood carving goes back to Boy Scout days, when I decided to make a neckerchief slide and to do so carved a wooden duck. I was probably then about thirteen years old. Various people later urged me to mount my carvings on plywood backgrounds and sell them as plaques. I continued to do carvings right up through high school. I simply abandoned it while in college and didn't start again until the late 1960s.

Dr. Emmett Blake was a mammalogist and ornithologist who had retired from the University of Nebraska the year before I arrived, and I replaced him. After he died in 1969, an estate auction was held. I went to the auction because I had heard there might be an Audubon *Quadrupeds* print among his effects. There was, and I was lucky enough to win the bid. The auction also included six beautiful mallard decoys. While looking at them, I noticed that another person, a sign painter named Ralph Stutheit, was also admiring them. Neither of us won the bid, but after sharing our disappointments, we decided to start carving decoys together, using his power tools and my access to museum specimens. That was the beginning of what became the Central Flyway Decoy Carvers and Collectors Club in 1970.

From then until the early 1980s I continued to make decoys and decorative carvings, until I had done about sixty of them. My carving was a wintertime activity, almost entirely done when I couldn't get down to campus to write and felt I needed something physical to do. I also rationalized that I was learning a little about bird anatomy as a result of carving them. Through the carving club I met many non-university people. Several first-class carvers emerged from our decoy-carving classes. These included Cliff Hollestelle, whom I helped teach how to make his first decoy. He later won at least one world championship for his carving and also produced many wonderful bronze sculptures.

In 1975 the club put on a major exhibit of classic antique decoys at the Sheldon Art Gallery at UNL, and I produced a catalog of the exhibit that was published in 1976 by the University of Nebraska Press (*The Bird Decoy: An American Art Form*). As the result of its inclusion in a later folk-art exhibit, a life-size preening trumpeter swan carving of mine was purchased by the gallery for its permanent collection. The gallery's then-curator, George Neubert, told me later that he considered it to have been one of his ten most important acquisitions during his tenure and thought it to be in the same league as a Brancusi.

Some of the other art exhibits that I have curated include three at the Great Plains Art Museum in Lincoln. The first was a 2002 exhibit titled "Migrations of the Imagination" with Lincoln photographer Mike Forsberg, using his photos and my drawings and carvings. In 2004 Bob Gress, a Kansas wildlife photographer, and I assembled an exhibit of drawings and photos celebrating the bicentennial of the Lewis and Clark expedition. In 2009, with the help of three friends who had accompanied me to the Galapagos Islands, I assembled an exhibit celebrating Charles Darwin's 200th birthday and the 150th anniversary of his *On the Origin of Species*.

Teaching

For the first ten or fifteen years I enjoyed teaching enormously, even though I taught large (150–200 students) classes of general zoology, year after year, and two sessions per semester. That was extremely time consuming, but it was nevertheless rewarding. I was determined to be the first person in the School of Biological Sciences to win the university's Distinguished Teaching Award. At that time the university was annually giving only two of these awards (including $500 and an inscribed medal), so they were highly coveted. That happened in 1968, the same year I was promoted to full professor. I received my promotion to full professor after I had been at UNL for six years. I think that was perhaps a university record too, and I haven't since heard of any UNL faculty member advancing from instructor to full professor within that time span.

In 1980 I was named Foundation Regents Professor of Biological Sciences. The other major university award I received was the Outstanding Research and Creativity Award, the university's highest faculty award (I think it included $10,000 plus a medal). I was the first person in the School of Biological Sciences to receive that award, in 1984.

It was very important, early on, to be a good teacher. Over the years, I hoped that I was influencing at least some of the vast numbers of students (about seven thousand) who went through my classes, and many did go on to find careers in medicine or graduate school. I developed an honors section for my General Zoology class, and at least one of its early members went on to obtain a PhD and full professorship at the University of Kansas. Eventually, my teaching interests began to wear down, and I was getting much more enjoyment out of writing. As I became more involved in writing, the responsibilities of teaching became more intrusive. In 1988, when I had a heart attack, I was working on seven or eight books.

During my forty years at UNL, twelve of my graduate students finished a PhD, and thirteen finished MS degrees. Roger Sharpe, my first graduate student, later taught biology for four decades at University of Nebraska–Omaha and was a coauthor of the first comprehensive book on the birds of Nebraska (2002).

The appearance on campus of Tom Mangelsen in 1969 was serendipitous for both of us. He had just graduated with a BS degree from Doane College and was at high risk of being drafted at the height of the Vietnam War. Although I already had a full load of four graduate students, I accepted his admission, mostly because he reminded me of my earlier self, and also because he mentioned during our first meeting that his father owned a hunting cabin on the Platte near Wood River. When he enrolled in my ornithology course in the following spring of 1970 we began spending time in duck blinds on the Platte, photographing all the waterfowl and cranes that strayed within range of our cameras. Tom later went with me on photographic trips to the Pacific Northwest and New Mexico, and eventually became one of the foremost wildlife photographers in the world. Since then he has published several books, and he lets me use some of his photos in some my books. We have collaborated on two recent books, the first on the natural history of the Yellowstone ecoregion (2014) and the second on the ecology and natural history of the cranes of the world (2015).

One of my most notable graduate students was Mary Bomberger (now Mary Bomberger Brown), who in 1980 undertook a study of the nesting ecology of Wilson's phalaropes at Crescent Lake National Wildlife Refuge, working out of Cedar Point Biological Station. In 1982 Professor Charles Brown of Tulsa University began a study of the ecology and social behavior of cliff swallows and was also working at Cedar Point. Mary joined in Charles's study after finishing her MS in 1982. Their work eventually resulted in several papers and a major monograph on the adaptations for and adaptive trade-offs associated with colonial nesting in the cliff swallow. In recognition of this research, they shared in the American Ornithologists' Union's Brewster Award in 2009, the highest honor for research given by that prestigious organization. In 2013 Mary and I cowrote a book on the birds of Nebraska's central Platte River valley. She is now on the faculty of the University of Nebraska and has done extensive field research on piping plovers in the Platte valley.

My last female graduate student, Jacqueline Canterbury, started an MS program with me in 2000 after finishing a biology undergraduate degree at Evergreen State College and the University of Washington. She later spent ten years doing bird research for the U.S. Forest Service on the Tongass National Forest. When starting at UNL, she asked me to be her supervisor for an MS degree that would emphasize wildlife conservation. She developed a conservation strategy for Nebraska's nongame birds for her MS thesis. She remained at UNL for a PhD but because I was soon to retire I decided I couldn't be her supervisor. I did serve as an unofficial advisor for her research on vocalizations in the yellow-breasted chat.

After finishing her PhD program in 2007, Jackie taught for several years at Wesleyan University in Lincoln, and still later taught at Sheridan College in Wyoming. In 2013 we coauthored a book on the birds of Wyoming's Bighorn Mountains, using an earlier booklet on the region's birds by Helen Downing as a starting point. Jackie retired from teaching in 2015 but left a lasting legacy for Nebraska by selling her marvelous riverside Niobrara River valley property to the Nebraska Game and Parks Commission and the U.S. Forest Service rather than selling it to a commercial developer. It will provide public access to the Niobrara River and nearly six hundred acres of bird-rich riparian woodland and meadows as Chat Canyon Wildlife Management Area.

Although I was never her formal teacher, I'm proud of my association with Allison Johnson. I first encountered her during an informal talk on cranes that I presented at Kearney in early 2003, in celebration of the completion of a visitor center at Audubon's Rowe Sanctuary. During my talk I noticed that a teenage girl sitting at a table nearest my speaker stand was paying no attention to me or the photos I was projecting but rather appeared to be deeply engrossed in drawing. After my talk I walked past her chair and saw that she had drawn a tiny but remarkably precise and accurate pencil sketch of a leopard on a tree limb. I then decided I had to meet her. Later, at the evening banquet, I walked over to her, introduced myself to her and her parents, and gave her a copy of one of my crane books. I also said I would like to help her in her academic pursuits (she was then a sophomore in high school) if I could.

A chance came soon thereafter when I was working on a series of about twenty drawings of the plants and animals discovered by Lewis and Clark during their 1804–6 expedition up the Missouri River to the Pacific. The drawings were to be part of a bicentennial celebration sponsored by the Center for Great Plains Studies and included in a related book that I was writing, and would later become part of the collection of the Great Plains Art Museum. I soon decided the drawings should be colored, and since I had neither the time nor talent to do them myself, I asked Allison if she would take on the task. My friends were astonished that I would turn over my drawings to a high school student, who said she had little experience in using colored pencils. However, I knew she would perform admirably, as indeed she did.

She, her parents, and I later spent time watching and photographing cranes, and I kept in occasional touch with her. In 2006 I decided to take some friends with me on a trip to the Galapagos the following year, in preparation of a bicentennial symposium and celebration of Charles Darwin's birth and work. When one of the people who intended to go had to drop out, I thought about inviting Allison, although I doubted that her parents would allow it. Luckily, they had no reservations, and Allison leapt at the chance. She did several paintings while we were there and helped to illustrate both the art exhibit and the booklet that I wrote in conjunction with the Darwin symposium. After graduating from St. Olaf College in Minnesota in 2010, Allison began graduate work in evolutionary biology at the University of Chicago and expects to complete her PhD there in 2016.

Another recent rewarding association that I have had has been with Dr. Karine Gil-Weir, a Venezuelan national who had finished a PhD at Texas Tech University, doing research on the population dynamics of whooping cranes. I met her in 2007 at the Whooping Crane Trust near Grand Island, where she was doing demographic research on sandhill and whooping cranes, and organizing a Whooper Watch program for tracking whooping crane migrations in Nebraska. Our interests strongly overlapped; I have helped edit several of her manuscripts, and we have collaborated on writing two articles on sandhill and whooping crane populations. Karine and her husband Enrique also translated my book *Crane Music* into Spanish (*Musica de las Grullas*) in 2014. Karine obtained her American citizenship in 2015.

My last PhD student, Josef Kren, was probably the best of all my teaching assistants and had already earned a doctoral degree from the Czech Republic by the time he arrived in Nebraska. He did his research on cowbird parasitism of red-winged blackbirds in western Nebraska and has been an active bird-bander and photographer. We have remained friends since his graduation in 1996, especially for birding and nature photography excursions. After some additional training in a Grenada medical school, Josef eventually became chairman of the Biology Department of Lincoln's Bryan Hospital's teaching program and has continued field research on western meadowlark vocalizations.

Cedar Point Biological Station: 1978–1993, 2008

Cedar Point Biological Station in Keith County, Nebraska, has been one of the wonderful educational opportunities that happened to the School of Biological Sciences, and also to me personally. The University of Nebraska obtained Cedar Point quite unexpectedly. One of our faculty, Gary Hergenrader, learned about the availability of the facility (a one-time Girl Scout camp) one summer while he was on a limnology field trip with students at Lake McConaughy. He somehow made the right contacts at UNL to convince the administration to lease the place for a few years. At that time I had never seen Lake

McConaughy or visited the biological station. When the university began a teaching program at the station in 1976, I was deeply involved in writing several books and didn't want to drive to western Nebraska to teach summer classes. Brent Nickol, our first Cedar Point director, kept after me, and in 1978 he convinced me to teach ornithology there for one session.

Thus, quite reluctantly, I packed my car and drove out there. Even while driving through Ogallala I was depressed about what a miserable summer this would be. Then I drove down the long hill leading to Kingsley Dam. At the bottom of the hill I turned east onto a dirt road (that no longer exists) and was suddenly at the bottom of a deep canyon filled with junipers and cottonwoods. I heard rock wrens singing loudly from the rocky slopes, and a group of screaming magpies flew by when a great horned owl suddenly took off from a rocky promontory. Like Dorothy landing in Oz, I thought I had suddenly been transported to a magical place. I fell in love with the area at that moment and went back to teach every summer for sixteen of the seventeen following summers.

I also returned to Cedar Point in the summer of 2008 to teach and also to compare changes in the station facilities (much better), the bird diversity and populations (worse), and the overall local environment and habitat quality (much worse). Cedar Point provided the most rewarding teaching in my career. As part of my final ornithology course in 2008 I assigned my eighteen students the immense job of summarizing forty years of Christmas Bird Count data for more than two hundred Great Plains bird species. I published the results as a UNL DigitalCommons monograph in 2009 and later wrote a more general book in 2015, to provide evidence as to how winter Great Plains bird populations have responded to recent global warming.

Cedar Point is a significantly better learning environment for those who want to learn field ornithology than is the Lincoln campus. My emphasis at Cedar Point was field ornithology rather than a lot of relatively dry lectures about those same subjects. Students work harder, I gave them higher grades, and I'm sure they enjoyed the course much more. Cedar Point became an integral part of my summer activities from the late 1970s to the early 1990s. I also did as much writing as I could do at Cedar Point. I would take out as many books or references as I could and write as much as possible there. Cedar Point is useful for sitting back and thinking about what I might want to write, doing drawings, and enjoying the birds. I spent more time watching birds during those few weeks than I did at any other time of the year.

Health

I had a heart attack in early November 1984. That happened as I arrived at Manter Hall at about 7:00 a.m., during the first bitterly cold day of that fall. I had pain going up the steps of Manter, and I took an aspirin, which might have saved my life. I went into my lab to get water for the aspirin and then collapsed on the floor. Luckily my grad student Sally Gaines was already at work in the lab, and she called 911.

I didn't realize I was possibly dying at the time. But, as I lay in the hospital, I decided that I didn't know how much more time I might have. I hoped to live at least a few more years, as I wanted to finish all the books I was working on. I had about eight unfinished books at that time.

The doctors said I had to recuperate at home for five or six weeks, and that just worked out perfectly. I had suffered the heart attack about five weeks before the end of fall semester classes, so the university officials decided I might just as well stay out through Christmas vacation. To celebrate my release from the hospital, I started carving a full-size flying trumpeter swan, which took about a week. I then decided to begin work on a new book. I started writing my *Birds of the Rocky Mountains* on our Apple IIe computer and had the manuscript well underway by the time I began teaching again in January.

I delayed my quintuple bypass surgery until 1988, when my doctor said it had become imperative to have it done. I had postponed bypass surgery about five years because our retired department chair, Dr. Harold Manter, had died during bypass surgery some years previously.

Thus, I went into the surgery ready for the worst, but when I woke up I felt euphoric. I was released five days later, which was then a very short release time. I had decided in the hospital that I had to come up with a new big project to get started on. I began work on my book on pelicans and cormorants of the world the day I got out of the hospital. Our herpetologist, John Lynch, saw me in my office that weekend, and he couldn't believe that I wasn't still in the hospital.

Since then I have had a stent placed in an artery, and a carotid artery clean-out (endarterectomy), but otherwise have been remarkably healthy.

Hunting and Photography

I had a paper route from about twelve years of age until I was in eighth grade. Then I started working in the meat department of a local supermarket, and I soon saved enough money to buy a used shotgun. I started going hunting with my dad and my older brother Keith when I was about fourteen years old. Dad was mostly a pheasant hunter, but I became much more interested in duck hunting. I hunted ducks until I was about sixteen years old. I then decided I would much rather try to photograph birds than shoot them, so I sold my shotgun to obtain a camera. I bought an Argus C-3, but not long afterward my mother borrowed it to take along on a trip, and it was stolen. She said she would replace it with a camera of my choice, which allowed me to buy my first camera with interchangeable lenses.

My "new" camera was an old (late 1930s) 35mm Kine Exakta I, a German-made single-lens reflex. My telephoto lens was an uncoated 180mm f/6.3 Zeiss Tessar. This very early single-lens reflex lacked a prism viewfinder, had no instant-return mirror, no motor drive, and no automatic shutter or auto-focusing lens. These early reflex cameras lacked prism viewfinders, so a person had to look down from above to focus. Trying to photograph a flying bird would require sheer luck to find its image, since it was both reversed and upside down. As soon as I could locate a bird in the vertical viewfinder I would snap the shutter without trying first to focus. I usually exposed at f/16 and 1/1000 of a second, using fast black-and-white film (Tri-X) and with the focus preset to about thirty yards. My average success rate was getting one or two frames (out of a 36-exposure roll of film) that had something in them more than empty sky.

Once I started photographing waterfowl, I would borrow my dad's car on spring weekends and drive about thirty miles south to the Lake Traverse area in South Dakota. I spent magical hours wading the shallow reed-lined marshes and watching endless flocks of migrating Canada, snow, and white-fronted geese fly overhead. I think that experience, more than anything else, made waterfowl my first love.

I gave up hunting during that period for two reasons. First, it strongly interfered with my photography, and I had far more pleasure in watching and photographing wild animals than in trying to kill them. I also became increasingly distraught by hunters who shot at anything they could see, and while in the field I often saw dead and wounded birds. The event that finally turned me fully away from hunting was when my older brother returned from the army. I was then about seventeen years old. We each bought deer licenses, and I went out deer hunting for the first time. Together we shot at, and one of us wounded, a doe. It was just dying when we reached it. Watching it die was something I couldn't bear, and I sold that gun immediately.

The last time that I purposefully killed a bird occurred when I was a graduate student at Washington State College. George Hudson, the curator of the Conner Museum, insisted that while I was doing my fieldwork I collect some birds for the museum's skin collection. Because Dr. Hudson was on my graduate committee, I had to comply with his request. Shooting into a brood of teal while the mother was frantically trying to protect them was the last time I ever used a shotgun.

I do have several friends who are hunters, so I have a nuanced attitude, based on what I think of that person and how he or she approaches hunting. If it weren't for hunting, I wouldn't have spent nearly so much time as a youngster in marshes, and I wouldn't have gone on memorable hunting trips with my older brother, my father, or my uncles. So, I have a strong identification with those social values of hunting. But it's a continuing problem for me to rationalize that against the pain that hunting causes, for no real reason other than entertainment.

For some species, hunting clearly doesn't damage their populations, if they are in good habitat. But I have real problems with hunting species such as cranes and swans, which are long-lived birds having extended pair bonds and fairly limited potential for population increase. So there is a biological rationale against hunting those species.

One of my strongest pieces of antihunting writing is a chapter in *Song of the North Wind* that describes the killing of snow geese along the periphery of Sand Lake National Wildlife Refuge. I had been watching birds being shot and wounded by hunters stationed along the roadsides and ditches around the edges of DeSoto National Wildlife Refuge. I also saw many wounded geese that had somehow managed to reach the refuge, where coyotes or eagles would probably later kill them. When visiting the Sand Lake refuge in 2015, I noted with satisfaction that hunting is no longer allowed from nearby roadsides or ditches.

Conservation Efforts

I don't write much about environmental crises. Much of what I try to say about the environment is done on a positive note. Species are worth preserving just for their very existence. The message of biodiversity is something that I feel is valuable as such, and that species of any kind are valuable and worth saving. That's a fairly easy message to give. My prairie dog book, *Prairie Dog Empire*, was largely a conservation sermon, and *Dragons and Unicorns* had a similar although hidden message. Indeed, nearly all my recent books touch on the issue of conservation, as do various popular writings, such as *A Prairie's Not Scary*, a poem on prairie ecology and conservation that I wrote and illustrated for Spring Creek Prairie Audubon Center.

I've testified on environmental issues only a few times and think my message is best transmitted through the reading public. I've never thought of myself as a figurehead for conservation, although I have won conservation awards from the American Ornithologists' Union, Nebraska Wildlife Federation, National Wildlife Federation, National Audubon Society, Nebraska Partnership for All-Bird Conservation, and other environmental or nature groups.

The passage of the Endangered Species Act, Clean Water Act, and Clean Air Act in the 1970s was a decisive step in the development of the modern conservation movement. The laws provided hard evidence that the federal government was finally moving on major environmental issues. But it's been pretty much downhill since 1980. There are now countless international and internal problems, fiscal deficits, and endless social issues facing us. I doubt we will ever be able to work nationally on the environmental issues and direct much money and attention to them, owing to the incredible waste of money and natural resources spent on ill-advised and non-winnable foreign wars.

I don't see the United States being able to continue to restore species the way we were thinking we were going to be able to with the Endangered Species Act in the 1970s. With the high corn prices of the past decade, the amount of native grasslands plowed up and converted to corn agriculture represents an area equal to the size of a small state. The inevitable drop in corn prices has resulted in economic hardship for farmers, together with destroyed native grassland ecosystems.

I think our choices are sort of like triage—to decide which species can be saved and do our best to save them, while the ones that are beyond saving will eventually disappear. That is highly depressing.

Religious Beliefs

I still get chills along my spine when I watch flocks of geese or cranes at sunset. That kind of experience still affects me just as much as it ever did. I think watching birds is the most spiritually rewarding thing I do these days. Occasionally a wonderful orchestra will give me those same chills, or some other great musical performance. Those are about the only two things that enthrall me in the sense of a being totally emotionally captured.

Somebody once told me that my dragons and unicorn book was being shelved under "Eastern Religions" in a bookstore, so there must be something remotely religious in that work. Basically I would describe myself as an atheist (literally, "lacking religion"), or occasionally as an agnostic ("without knowledge of God"). I am attracted to the mystical, the unknown. I don't give the seemingly supernatural a name, but I like a sense of mystery. I would never suggest there is a universal or personal god somewhere, but it's nice to think of the natural world as, in some ways, still being mysterious.

Embracing mystery is counter to science, and I suppose that's an anomaly in my thinking. Perhaps it's part of going back to the Native American concept of an overall natural spirit, even though one may not care to give that spirit a name. I am still attracted to the idea that life is so diverse and interesting it is appropriate that there are some things we can't totally understand and perhaps will always be beyond our knowledge. There is still a mystery to life that I find appealing to think about, and a value to life beyond the obvious. It is that kind of inexplicable wonder that in my view is sacred, rather than cathedrals, churches, or other religious symbols.

I believe that the various formal religious belief systems of the world have gotten humanity into far more trouble than they are worth. I think science can be an adequate substitute for organized religions, so far as satisfying pervasive human needs for some sort of belief system. Science is fallible, and so I'm sure that science will never provide us with all the answers we would like to have. Yet, I would strongly recommend it over religion.

That said, I have been a member of the Unitarian Church since 1975, which seems counter to my just-stated beliefs. But that church does not demand a belief in the supernatural and instead is centered on a humanistic approach to life and a broad tolerance of other religious and philosophic views. In fact, when I joined the church I asked the then-pastor Rev. Charles Stephen if he would mind adding an atheist to its roles. He laughed and told me not to worry, as there were certainly already several such nonbelievers within the church's membership. I then realized I had finally found a church in which I could be comfortable.

Summary of Recognitions and Awards

Academic Honors and Awards

I have been listed in *American Men and Women of Science, Who's Who in the Midwest, Contemporary Authors, The Writers Directory*, and so forth. I was named Outstanding Alumnus of North Dakota State University in 1996. I have been an honorary life member of the Nebraska Ornithologists' Union since 1984 and an elected Fellow of the American Ornithologists' Union since 1961. I have been a Guggenheim Foundation Fellow (1972) and have held overseas postdoctoral fellowships from the National Science Foundation (1959–60) and the U.S. Public Health Service (1960–61). I was the first University of Nebraska faculty member to win all three major faculty awards. I was given the Distinguished Teaching Award and Outstanding Research and Creative Activity Award, and I was named a University Foundation Professor.

Humanitarian Honors

I was named by the *Lincoln Journal Star* (July 15, 1999) as one of "100 people who have helped build Nebraska—politically, economically, socially or physically—the past 100 years." I was also selected by the *Omaha World-Herald* (November 29, 1999) as one of "100 outstanding Nebraskans of the twentieth century." A total of thirty persons (only six of whom were then still alive) were included in both lists, and since then some have died.

In 2003 I was inducted into the Ak-Sar-Ben Court of Honor.

Ak-Sar-Ben (Nebraska spelled in reverse), an Omaha-based philanthropic organization, bestows this honor to only four Nebraskans each year. In December 2009 I received an Honorary Doctor of Science degree from UNL and delivered the undergraduate commencement address.

In 2014 Dr. Everett Madson, a former undergraduate student, gave a collection of 160 bird taxidermy specimens in my name to the Nebraska State Museum. This gift seemed a somewhat ironic honor, considering my current thoughts on sport hunting, but I made the best of it by writing a small book describing all of the ninety game-bird species in the collection.

Literary Awards

My literary awards include the Wildlife Society's annual award for the outstanding book or monograph in the field of terrestrial wildlife biology, awarded in 1973 to *Grouse and Quails of North America*. The *Library Journal* selected *Waterfowl: Their Biology and Natural History* as one of the most outstanding books of the year in science and technology. In 1988 I received the Loren Eiseley Award from Omaha's Clarkson Hospital, given for writings that blend science with humanism, and the Mari Sandoz Award was given to me in 1984 by the Nebraska Library Association for contributions to the literature of Nebraska. My *Yellowstone Wildlife: Ecology and Natural History of the Greater Yellowstone Ecosystem* won the 2014 Nonfiction (Natural History) Award by the Nebraska Center for the Book, as did my *Nature of Nebraska* in 2002.

Conservation Awards

In 2001 the Nebraska section of the National Audubon Society honored me with its Fred Thomas Nebraska Steward Award, and in the same year the Nebraska Wildlife Federation presented me with a Lifetime Achievement Award. In 2005 I received the National Wildlife

Federation's National Conservation Achievement Award (Science), given annually to a scientist who has performed conservation work of national significance. In 2007 I received the President's Award from the Nebraska Partnership for All-Bird Conservation. In 2008 the National Audubon Society awarded me the Charles H. Callison Award, their highest honor, awarded by the society for volunteer conservation work. In 2012 I received the American Ornithologists' Union's Ralph Schreiber Award (*Auk* 130 [2013]:205–6) for "extraordinary scientific contributions to the conservation, restoration, or preservation of birds and their habitats."

Publishing Activities

Since 1955 I have largely concentrated my research on the comparative biology of several major bird groups of the world, having published nine world monographs (waterfowl; grouse; cranes; shorebirds; pheasants; quails, partridges and francolins; bustards, hemipodes, and sandgrouse; cormorants, darters, and pelicans; and trogons and quetzals). Six of my monographs are on various North American bird groups (waterfowl; grouse and quails; auks, loons, and grebes; owls; hawks, eagles, and falcons; hummingbirds). I have also written or coauthored monographs on the stiff-tailed ducks (*Ruddy Ducks and Other Stifftails*), sexual selection in arena-breeding birds (*Arena Birds*), and avian social parasitism (*The Avian Brood Parasites*).

Seven of my larger books describe Nebraska's natural history: *The Platte: Channels in Time*, *This Fragile Land: A Natural History of the Nebraska Sandhills*, *The Nature of Nebraska: Ecology and Biodiversity*, *The Niobrara: A River Running through Time*, *Nebraska's Wetlands: Their Wildlife and Ecology*, and *Seasons of the Tallgrass Prairie: A Nebraska Year*.

I have also written or coauthored six hard-copy books on regional ornithology: *Birds of the Great Plains*, *Birds of the Central Platte River Valley and Adjacent Counties*, *The Birds of Nebraska and Adjacent Plains States*, *Rocky Mountain Birds: Birds and Birding in the Central and*

Northern Rockies, and *Birds and Birding in Wyoming's Bighorn Mountains Region.*

Four of my hard-copy books concern Great Plains and Rocky Mountains ecology and natural history: *Great Wildlife of the Great Plains, Faces of the Great Plains, Teton Wildlife: Observations by a Naturalist,* and *Yellowstone Wildlife: Ecology and Natural History of the Greater Yellowstone Ecosystem.*

Although I have written on relatively technical subjects ever since graduate school, it was not until twenty years later that I ventured into writing in a more literary style and attempted to reach a much broader audience. This was marked by the 1974 Doubleday publication of my *Song of the North Wind: A Story of the Snow Goose.* In 1981 St. Martin's Press published my *Dragons and Unicorns: A Natural History,* coauthored with my daughter Karin. This book is an allegorical and whimsical view of the natural world, with an underlying conservation message. It has remained continuously in print. *Earth, Water, and Sky: A Naturalist's Stories and Sketches* (1999) consists of previously published essays and stories of personal bird observations throughout the world.

In 2013 I collaborated with photographer and friend Thomas Mangelsen on an illustrated book (photographs and drawings) on the natural history of the greater Yellowstone region, and we followed this with a similar book on the cranes of North America and the Old World (2015). One of my popular books, *Those of the Gray Wind: The Sandhill Cranes,* was the basis for developing a documentary film of the same title (*Cranes of the Grey Wind*) with Tom Mangelsen, which I partly wrote.

Seasons of the Tallgrass Prairie: A Nebraska Year (2014) is a collection of Nebraska-based essays from the newspaper *Prairie Fire.* I helped edit and also contributed the foreword and three essays in a similar collection of *Prairie Fire* essays in 2015 (*Natural Treasures of the Great Plains: An Ecological Perspective*). My 1991 book *Crane Music* was translated into Spanish in 2014, and other books that have also been translated include *Song of the North Wind* (Russian, Latvian) and *Those of the Gray Wind* (Chinese).

Collectively, my nearly seventy hard-copy books occupy almost six feet of bookshelf space, include about thirteen thousand pages of text, and contain a conservative estimate of at least 2.5 million words. Additionally, I have written many extended manuscripts that were published as electronic books with the University of Nebraska–Lincoln's DigitalCommons (fourteen books or booklets and more than one hundred electronically archived papers and articles). As of 2015, these had been downloaded more than two hundred thousand times and are accessible worldwide. I have published more than 100 journal papers, book chapters, or other reviewed manuscripts, and over 150 articles, essays, and nontechnical writings. I am thus probably the world's most prolific living author of ornithological and natural history literature.

Art and Other Creative Activities

Besides writing, nearly all of my books have been personally illustrated, using either line drawings or photographs. More than a thousand of my drawings have been published, as well as over two hundred color or black-and-white photographs. Several of my drawings and wooden bird sculptures are in private collections or museums.

In conjunction with a University of Nebraska Sheldon Gallery exhibit of antique hunting decoys that I organized, I edited and cowrote a book (1976) on hand-carved decoys as folk art. I also wrote (1998) a book describing thirty-six George M. Sutton portraits of baby birds, housed in the rare book collection of Chicago's Field Museum of Natural History.

In 2001 the Center for Great Plains Studies at the University of Nebraska published a booklet that I wrote (*Migrations of the Imagination*) to accompany an exhibit of my drawings and sculptures at the Great Plains Art Museum in Lincoln. I published a book in 2003 on the natural history of the Lewis and Clark expedition in the Great Plains (*Lewis and Clark on the Great Plains: A Natural History*) to accompany an associated bicentennial 2004 art exhibit I developed and curated for the Great Plains Art Museum in Lincoln, and in 2008 I curated an exhibit there celebrating Charles Darwin's 200th birthday, titled "Celebrating Darwin's Legacy: Evolution in the Galapagos Islands and the Great Plains."

In 1989 Nebraska Public Television produced a half-hour documentary about me titled *A Passion for Birds*, and in 2008 NETV produced a sixty-minute program, *Crane Song*, based in part on my *Crane Music* book.

Sandhill cranes

Curriculum vitae

(updated through June 2015)

Academic History

1953	BS (Zoology), North Dakota State University
1955	MS (Wildlife Management), Washington State University
1959	PhD (Vertebrate Zoology), Cornell University
1959–61	Postdoctoral Fellow (NSF and NIH), Bristol University (England)
1961–62	Instructor, Department of Zoology, University of Nebraska
1962–65	Assistant Professor with Tenure, Department of Zoology, University of Nebraska
1965–68	Associate Professor, Department of Zoology and Physiology, University of Nebraska–Lincoln
1968–80	Professor, School of Biological Sciences, University of Nebraska–Lincoln
1980–2001	Foundation Regents Professor, School of Biological Sciences, University of Nebraska–Lincoln
2001–present	Foundation Regents Professor Emeritus, School of Biological Sciences, University of Nebraska–Lincoln

Websites

Paul Johnsgard's Books. (Summary of books published through 2003.) http://pauljohnsgardbooks.tripod.com/

Paul A. Johnsgard. Nebraska Center for Writers (summary of Nebraska writing). http://mockingbird.creighton.edu/NCW/johnsgar.htm

Paul Johnsgard: Comprehensive Vita and Bibliography (vita through 2012). http://digitalcommons.unl.edu/biosciornithology/25/

Papers in the Biological Sciences—Paul Johnsgard Collection (150+ articles, chapters, essays, etc.). http://digitalcommons.unl.edu/johnsgard/

Books Published in Hard-Copy Format

Throughout, titles marked with asterisks can be accessed at the
University of Nebraska–Lincoln DigitalCommons at
http://digitalcommons.unl.edu/

Handbook of Waterfowl Behavior. 1965. Ithaca, NY: Cornell University Press. 378 pp.* http://digitalcommons.unl.edu/bioscihandwaterfowl/15/

Animal Behavior. 1967, 1972 (2nd ed.). Dubuque, IA: William Brown. 156 pp.

Waterfowl: Their Biology and Natural History. 1968. Lincoln: University of Nebraska Press. 138 pp.

Grouse and Quails of North America. 1973. Lincoln: University of Nebraska Press. 553 pp.* http://digitalcommons.unl.edu/bioscigrouse/1/

Song of the North Wind: A Story of the Snow Goose. 1974. New York: Doubleday. 150 pp. Reprinted 1979, University of Nebraska Press. Translated into Russian (1977) and Latvian (1980).*
http://digitalcommons.unl.edu/biosciornithology/50/

North American Game Birds of Upland and Shoreline. 1975. Lincoln: University of Nebraska Press. 183 pp.

Waterfowl of North America. 1975. Bloomington: Indiana University Press. 573 pp.* http://digitalcommons.unl.edu/biosciwaterfowlna/1/

The Bird Decoy: An American Art Form. 1976. Lincoln: University of Nebraska Press. 188 pp.

Ducks, Geese, and Swans of the World. 1978. Lincoln: University of Nebraska Press. 400 pp.* http://digitalcommons.unl.edu/biosciducksgeeseswans/1/

Birds of the Great Plains: Breeding Species and Their Distribution. 1979. Lincoln: University of Nebraska Press. 538 pp.*
http://digitalcommons.unl.edu/bioscibirdsgreatplains/1/

A Guide to North American Waterfowl. 1979. Bloomington: Indiana University Press. 270 pp.

The Plovers, Sandpipers, and Snipes of the World. 1981. Lincoln: University of Nebraska Press. 492 pp.

Those of the Gray Wind: The Sandhill Cranes. 1981. New York: St. Martin's Press. Reprinted (1987), University of Nebraska Press. Translated into Chinese (1996). 150 pp.

Teton Wildlife: Observations by a Naturalist. 1982. Boulder: Colorado Associated University Press. 128 pp.

Dragons and Unicorns: A Natural History. 1982. (With Karin Johnsgard.) New York: St. Martin's Press. 164 pp.

The Grouse of the World. 1983. Lincoln: University of Nebraska Press. 410 pp.

The Hummingbirds of North America. 1983. Washington, D.C.: Smithsonian Institution Press. 302 pp.

The Cranes of the World. 1983. Bloomington: Indiana University Press. 256 pp.*
http://digitalcommons.unl.edu/bioscicranes/1/

The Platte: Channels in Time. 1984. Lincoln: University of Nebraska Press. 176 pp.

Prairie Children, Mountain Dreams. 1985. Lincoln, NE: Media Publishing Co. 87 pp. (fiction)

The Pheasants of the World. 1986. Oxford, UK: Oxford University Press. 204 pp.

Birds of the Rocky Mountains with Particular Reference to National Parks in the Northern Rocky Mountain Region. 1986. Boulder: Colorado Associated University Press. 504 pp. Reprinted (1993), University of Nebraska Press.*
http://digitalcommons.unl.edu/bioscibirdsrockymtns/1/

Diving Birds of North America. 1987. Lincoln: University of Nebraska Press. 286 pp.* http://digitalcommons.unl.edu/bioscidivingbirds/1/

Waterfowl of North America: The Complete Ducks, Geese, and Swans. 1987. (With Robin Hill, S. Dillon Ripley, and the Duke of Edinburgh.) Augusta, GA: Morris. 135 pp. (species accounts)

The Quails, Partridges, and Francolins of the World. 1988. Oxford, UK: Oxford University Press. 264 pp.

North American Owls: Biology and Natural History. 1988. Washington, D.C.: Smithsonian Institution Press. 295 pp.*
http://digitalcommons.unl.edu/johnsgard/46/

Hawks, Eagles, and Falcons of North America: Biology and Natural History. 1990. Washington, D.C.: Smithsonian Institution Press. 403 pp.

Crane Music: A Natural History of American Cranes. 1991. Washington, D.C.: Smithsonian Institution Press. Reprinted (1997), University of Nebraska Press. 136 pp.

Bustards, Hemipodes, and Sandgrouse: Birds of Dry Places. 1991. Oxford, UK: Oxford University Press. 276 pp.

Ducks in the Wild: Conserving Waterfowl and Their Habitats. Toronto: Key-Porter (1992) and New York: Prentice Hall (1993). 158 pp.

Cormorants, Darters, and Pelicans of the World. 1993. Washington, D.C.: Smithsonian Institution Press. 445 pp.

Arena Birds: Sexual Selection and Behavior. 1994. Washington, D.C.: Smithsonian Institution Press. 330 pp.

This Fragile Land: A Natural History of the Nebraska Sandhills. 1995. Lincoln: University of Nebraska Press. 256 pp.

Ruddy Ducks and Other Stifftails: Their Behavior and Biology. (With Montserrat Carbonell.) 1996. Norman: University of Oklahoma Press. 284 pp.

The Avian Brood Parasites: Deception at the Nest. 1997. New York: Oxford University Press. 409 pp.

The Hummingbirds of North America. 1997. 2nd. ed. Washington, D.C.: Smithsonian Institution Press. 277 pp.

Baby Bird Portraits by George Miksch Sutton: Watercolors in the Field Museum. 1998. Norman: University of Oklahoma Press. 80 pp.

Earth, Water, and Sky: A Naturalist's Stories and Sketches. 1999. Austin: University of Texas Press. 157 pp.

The Pheasants of the World: Biology and Natural History. 1999. Washington, D.C.: Smithsonian Institution Press. 396 pp. (Revised version of the 1986 Oxford University Press edition.)

Trogons and Quetzals of the World. 2000. Washington, D.C.: Smithsonian Institution Press. 224 pp.

Prairie Birds: Fragile Splendor in the Great Plains. 2001. Lawrence: University Press of Kansas. 331 pp.

The Nature of Nebraska: Ecology and Biodiversity. 2001. Lincoln: University of Nebraska Press. 402 pp.

Grassland Grouse and Their Conservation. 2002. Washington, D.C.: Smithsonian Institution Press. 157 pp.

North American Owls: Biology and Natural History. 2002. 2nd expanded edition (including Mexico). Washington, D.C.: Smithsonian Institution Press. 298 pp.

Great Wildlife of the Great Plains. 2003. Lawrence: University Press of Kansas. 309 pp.

Lewis and Clark on the Great Plains: A Natural History. 2003. Lincoln: University of Nebraska Press. 143 pp.

Faces of the Great Plains: Prairie Wildlife. 2003. (With photographs and photographic notes by Bob Gress.) Lawrence: University Press of Kansas. 190 pp.

Prairie Dog Empire: A Saga of the Shortgrass Prairie. 2004. Lincoln: University of Nebraska Press. 142 pp.

The Niobrara: A River Running through Time. 2007. Lincoln: University of Nebraska Press. 374 pp.

Wind through the Buffalo Grass: A Lakota Story Cycle. 2008. Lincoln, NE: Plains Chronicles Press. 214 pp. (fiction)

Sandhill and Whooping Cranes: Ancient Voices over America's Wetlands. 2011. Lincoln: University of Nebraska Press. 155 pp.

Rocky Mountain Birds: Birds and Birding in the Central and Northern Rocky Mountains. 2011. Lincoln, NE: Zea Books (print) edition available from http://www.lulu.com/shop/paul-johnsgard/rocky-mountain-birds/paperback/product-18607006.html and University of Nebraska–Lincoln DigitalCommons (online) at http://digitalcommons.unl.edu/zeabook/7/. 274 pp.*

A Nebraska Bird-finding Guide. 2011. Lincoln, NE: Zea Books (print) edition available from http://www.lulu.com/shop/paul-johnsgard/a-nebraska-bird-finding-guide/paperback/product-21768130.html and University of Nebraska–Lincoln DigitalCommons (online) at http://digitalcommons.unl.edu/zeabook/5/, 166 pp.*

Wetland Birds of the Central Plains: South Dakota, Nebraska, and Kansas. 2012. Lincoln, NE: Zea Books (print) available from http://www.lulu.com/shop/paul-johnsgard/wetland-birds-of-the-central-plains-south-dakota-nebraska-and-kansas/paperback/product-18889896.html and University of Nebraska–Lincoln DigitalCommons (online) at http://digitalcommons.unl.edu/zeabook/8/. 275 pp.*

Nebraska's Wetlands: Their Wildlife and Ecology. 2012. Lincoln: Conservation and Survey Division, Institute of Agriculture and Natural Resources (IANR), University of Nebraska–Lincoln. *Water Survey Paper No. 78.* 202 pp.

Wings over the Great Plains: The Central Flyway. 2012. Zea Books (print) available from http://www.lulu.com/shop/paul-johnsgard/wings-over-the-great-plains-bird-migrations-in-the-central-flyway/paperback/product-20522789.html and University of Nebraska–Lincoln DigitalCommons (online) at http://digitalcommons.unl.edu/zeabook/13/. 249 pp.*

Birds of the Central Platte River Valley and Adjacent Counties. 2013. (With Mary B. Brown.) Lincoln, NE: Zea Books (print) available from http://www.lulu.com/shop/paul-a-johnsgard-and-mary-bomberger-brown/birds-of-the-central-platte-river-valley-and-adjacent-counties/paperback/product-20723724.html and University of Nebraska–Lincoln DigitalCommons (online) at http://digitalcommons.unl.edu/zeabook/15/. 182 pp.*

The Birds of Nebraska. 2013. Lincoln, NE: Zea Books (print) available from http://www.lulu.com/shop/paul-johnsgard/the-birds-of-nebraska-revised-edition-2013/paperback/product-21096798.html and University of

Nebraska–Lincoln DigitalCommons (online) at http://digitalcommons.unl. edu/zeabook/17/. (Revised several times since original 1980 edition.) Ca. 150 pp.*

Yellowstone Wildlife: Ecology and Natural History of the Greater Yellowstone Ecosystem. 2013. (Photos by Thomas D. Mangelsen.) Boulder: University Press of Colorado. 239 pp.

Birds and Birding in Wyoming's Bighorn Mountains Region. 2013. (With Jacqueline L. Canterbury and Helen F. Downing.) Lincoln, NE: Zea Books (print) available from http://www.lulu.com/shop/paul-a-johnsgard-and-jacqueline-l-canterbury-and-helen-f-downing/birds-and-birding-in-wyomings-bighorn-mountains-region/paperback/product-21777223.html and University of Nebraska–Lincoln DigitalCommons (online) at http://digitalcommons.unl.edu/zeabook/18/. 260 pp.*

Musica de las Grullas: Una Historia Natural de las Grullas de América. 2014. Spanish translation of *Crane Music* (1991 edition, updated to 2013). Translation by Enrique Weir and Karine Gil-Weir. Lincoln, NE: Zea Books (print) available from http://www.lulu.com/shop/paul-johnsgard-and-enrique-weir-and-karine-gil-weir/m%C3%BAsica-de-las-grullas/paperback/product-21789000.html and University of Nebraska–Lincoln DigitalCommons (online) at http://digitalcommons.unl.edu/zeabook/25/. 182 pp.*

Game Birds of the World: A Catalog of the Madson Collection. 2014. Lincoln: University of Nebraska School of Natural Resources and Nebraska State Museum. 96 pp.* http://digitalcommons.unl.edu/johnsgard/50/

Seasons of the Tallgrass Prairie: A Nebraska Year. 2014. Lincoln: University of Nebraska Press. 171 pp.

Global Warming and Population Responses among Great Plains Birds. 2015. Lincoln, NE: Zea Books (print) available from http://www.lulu.com/shop/ http://www.lulu.com/shop/paul-johnsgard/global-warming-and-population-responses-among-great-plains-birds/paperback/product-22063416. html and University of Nebraska–Lincoln DigitalCommons (online) at http://digitalcommons.unl.edu/zeabook/26/. 384 pp.*

Natural Treasures of the Great Plains: An Ecological Perspective. 2015. (Coeditor with T. Lynch and J. Phillips; author of foreword and three essays.) Lincoln, NE: Prairie Chronicles Press. 220 pp.

At Home and at Large in the Great Plains: Essays and Memories. 2015. Lincoln, NE: Zea Books.

A Chorus of Cranes: The Cranes of North America and the World. 2015. (With photographs by T. D. Mangelsen.) Boulder: University Press of Colorado.

Miscellaneous Original Books and Digital Reprints

Original Electronic Books and Papers

A Guide to the Natural History of the Central Platte Valley of Nebraska. 2007. *Papers in Ornithology.* Lincoln: University of Nebraska–Lincoln DigitalCommons. 156 pp.* http://digitalcommons.unl.edu/biosciornithology/40/

A Guide to the Tallgrass Prairies of Eastern Nebraska and Adjacent States. 2007. *Papers in Ornithology.* Lincoln: University of Nebraska–Lincoln Digital-Commons. 156 pp.* http://digitalcommons.unl.edu/biosciornithology/39/

Body Weights and Species Distributions of Birds in Nebraska's Central and Western Platte Valley. 2008. (With William C. Scharf, Josef Kren, and Linda R. Brown.) Lincoln: University of Nebraska–Lincoln DigitalCommons. *Papers in Ornithology.* 35 pp.*
http://digitalcommons.unl.edu/biosciornithology/43/

Cranes of the World in 2008: A Supplement to Crane Music. 2008. *Papers in Ornithology.* Lincoln: University of Nebraska–Lincoln DigitalCommons. 18 pp.* http://digitalcommons.unl.edu/biosciornithology/45/

Four Decades of Christmas Bird Counts in the Great Plains: Ornithological Evidence of a Changing Climate. 2009. (With range maps by Thomas Shane.) *Papers in Ornithology.* Lincoln: University of Nebraska–Lincoln DigitalCommons. 334 pp.* http://digitalcommons.unl.edu/biosciornithology/46/

Louis A. Fuertes and the Zoological Art of the 1926–1927 Abyssinian Expedition of the Field Museum of Natural History. 2009. Lincoln: University of Nebraska–Lincoln DigitalCommons. *Papers in Ornithology.* 121 pp.*
http://digitalcommons.unl.edu/biosciornithology/44/

Electronic Book Reprints

Grouse and Quails of North America. 2008. (1973 ed.) Lincoln: University of Nebraska–Lincoln DigitalCommons.*
http://digitalcommons.unl.edu/bioscigrouse/1/

Handbook of Waterfowl Behavior. 2008 (1965 ed.) Lincoln: University of Nebraska–Lincoln DigitalCommons.*
http://digitalcommons.unl.edu/bioscihandwaterfowl/7/

Birds of the Rocky Mountains with Particular Reference to National Parks in the Northern Rocky Mountain Region. 2009. (1986 ed., with a 2009 literature supplement). Lincoln: University of Nebraska–Lincoln DigitalCommons. 504+ pp.* http://digitalcommons.unl.edu/bioscibirdsrockymtns/1/

Birds of the Great Plains: Three Decades of Change in Great Plains Birds: A 2009 Supplement to The Birds of the Great Plains: Breeding Species and Their Distribution. 2009. (1979 ed. with a literature supplement and revised maps.) Lincoln: University of Nebraska–Lincoln DigitalCommons. 530+ pp.* http://digitalcommons.unl.edu/bioscibirdsgreatplains/6/

Song of the North Wind: A Story of the Snow Goose. 2009. (1974 ed., with a new afterword.) Lincoln: University of Nebraska–Lincoln DigitalCommons.* http://digitalcommons.unl.edu/biosciornithology/50/

Ducks, Geese, and Swans of the World. 2010. (1978 ed., with revised maps and a new supplement.) Lincoln: University of Nebraska–Lincoln DigitalCommons.* http://digitalcommons.unl.edu/biosciducksgeeseswans/1/

Waterfowl of North America. 2010. (1975 ed., with a 2009 literature supplement.) Lincoln: University of Nebraska–Lincoln DigitalCommons.* http://digitalcommons.unl.edu/biosciwaterfowlna/1/

North American Owls: Biology and Natural History. 2014. (1988 ed.) Washington, D.C.: Smithsonian Institution Press. 295 pp. Lincoln: University of Nebraska–Lincoln DigitalCommons.* http://digitalcommons.unl.edu/johnsgard/46/

Original Hard-copy Booklets

A Prairie's Not Scary. 2012. Lincoln: Zea Books (print) available from http://www.lulu.com/shop/paul-a-johnsgard/a-prairies-not-scary/paperback/product-18942332.html and University of Nebraska–Lincoln DigitalCommons (online) at http://digitalcommons.unl.edu/zeabook/10/. 48 pp.* (prairie poetry)

Migrations of the Imagination. 2002. Catalog of art exhibition curated by P. A. Johnsgard. Lincoln, NE: Center for Great Plains Studies. 32 pp.* http://digitalcommons.unl.edu/biosciornithology/48/

Prairie Suite: A Celebration. 2006. Poems by Twyla Hansen and drawings by P. A. Johnsgard. Denton, NE: Spring Creek Prairie Audubon Center. 64 pp.* http://digitalcommons.unl.edu/johnsgard/37

Celebrating Darwin's Legacy: Evolution in the Galapagos Islands and the Great Plains. 2009. Catalog of art exhibition curated by P. A. Johnsgard. Lincoln, NE: Center for Great Plains Studies. 32 pp.* http://digitalcommons.unl.edu/biosciornithology/47/

Thesis and Dissertation Titles

1955. Effects of water fluctuation and vegetation change on bird populations, especially waterfowl. MS thesis, Washington State University, Pullman, Washington.* http://digitalcommons.unl.edu/johnsgard/2/

1959. Evolutionary relationships among the North American mallards. PhD dissertation, Cornell University, Ithaca, New York.* http://digitalcommons.unl.edu/biosciornithology/62/

Journal Papers, Book Chapters, and other Longer Publications (100+)

1953 – *Waterfowl of North Dakota*. North Dakota Institute for Regional Studies, Fargo. 16 pp.* http://digitalcommons.unl.edu/biosciornithology/42/

1954 – Birds observed in the Potholes region during 1953–54. *Murrelet* 35:25–31.* http://digitalcommons.unl.edu/biosciornithology/64

1955 – Courtship activities of the Anatidae in eastern Washington. *Condor* 57:19–27.* http://digitalcommons.unl.edu/biosciornithology/66

1956 – Waterfowl sex ratios during spring in Washington State and their interpretation. (With I. O. Buss.) *Journal of Wildlife Management* 20:384–388.* http://digitalcommons.unl.edu/biosciornithology/67

– Effects of water fluctuation and vegetation change on bird populations, particularly waterfowl. *Ecology* 37:689–701.* http://digitalcommons.unl.edu/johnsgard/2

1957 – The relation of spring bird distribution to a vegetation mosaic in southeastern Washington. (With W. H. Rickard.) *Ecology* 38:171–174.* http://digitalcommons.unl.edu/johnsgard/3

1959 – Comments on species recognition with special reference to the Wood Duck and the Mandarin Duck. (with William C. Dilger) *Wilson Bulletin* 71:46–53.* http://digitalcommons.unl.edu/biosciornithology/11/

– An electrophoretic study of egg-white proteins in twenty-three breeds of domestic fowl. (With Charles G. Sibley.) *American Naturalist* 93:107–115.* http://digitalcommons.unl.edu/johnsgard/4

– Variability in the electrophoretic patterns of avian serum proteins (With C. G. Sibley.) *Condor* 61:85–95.* http://digitalcommons.unl.edu/biosciornithology/69

1960 – Hybridization in the Anatidae and its taxonomic implications. *Condor* 62:25–33.* http://digitalcommons.unl.edu/biosciornithology/71

– Comparative behavior of the Anatidae and its evolutionary implications. *Wildfowl Trust 11th Annual Report*, pp. 31–45.

– Pair-formation mechanisms in *Anas* (Anatidae) and related genera. *Ibis* 102:616–618. http://digitalcommons.unl.edu/johnsgard/5

– A quantitative study of sexual behavior of mallards and black ducks. *Wilson Bulletin* 72:133–155.* http://digitalcommons.unl.edu/biosciornithology/10

– The systematic position of ringed teal. *Bulletin British Ornithological Club* 80:165–167.

– Classification and evolutionary relationships of the sea ducks. *Condor* 62:426–437.* http://digitalcommons.unl.edu/biosciornithology/70

1961 – Evolutionary relationships among the North American mallards. *Auk* 78:1–43.* http://digitalcommons.unl.edu/biosciornithology/62

– The taxonomy of the Anatidae—a behavioural analysis. *Ibis* 103a:71–85.* http://digitalcommons.unl.edu/johnsgard/29

– The breeding biology of the magpie goose. *Wildfowl Trust 12th Annual Report*, pp. 92–103.

– The tracheal anatomy of the Anatidae and its taxonomic significance. *Wildfowl Trust 12th Annual Report*, pp. 58–69.

– The systematic position of the marbled teal. *Bulletin British Ornithological Club* 81:37–43.

– The sexual behavior and systematic position of the hooded merganser. *Wilson Bulletin* 73:227–236.* http://digitalcommons.unl.edu/biosciornithology/9

– Wintering distribution changes in mallards and black ducks. *American Midland Naturalist* 66:477–484.* http://digitalcommons.unl.edu/biosciornithology/72

1962 – Evolutionary trends in the behavior and morphology of the Anatidae. *Wildfowl Trust 13th Annual Report*, pp. 130–148.

1963 – Behavioral isolating mechanisms in the family Anatidae. *Proceedings of the 13th International Ornithological Congress*, pp. 531–543.* http://digitalcommons.unl.edu/johnsgard/23

1964 – Comparative behavior and relationships of the eiders. *Condor* 66:113–129.* http://digitalcommons.unl.edu/biosciornithology/63

– Observations on the breeding biology of the spectacled eider. *Wildfowl Trust 15th Annual Report*, pp. 104–107.

1965 – Observations on some aberrant Australian Anatidae. *Wildfowl Trust 16th Annual Report*, pp. 73–83.

156

1966 – Behavior of the Australian musk duck and blue-billed duck. *Auk* 83:98–110.* http://digitalcommons.unl.edu/biosciornithology/61

– The biology and relationships of the torrent duck. *Wildfowl Trust 17th Annual Report*, pp. 66–74.

– Inheritance of behavioral characters in F_2 mallard × pintail (*Anas platyrhynchos* L. × *Anas acuta* L.) hybrids. (With Roger S. Sharpe.) *Behaviour* 27(3–4): 259–272.* http://digitalcommons.unl.edu/johnsgard/7/

1967 – Sympatry changes and hybridization incidence in mallards and black ducks. *American Midland Naturalist* 77:51–63.* http://digitalcommons.unl.edu/biosciornithology/76

– Observations on the behavior and relationships of the white-backed duck and the stiff-tailed ducks. *Wildfowl Trust 18th Annual Report*, pp. 98–107.

1968 – Distributional changes and interactions between prairie chickens and sharp-tailed grouse in the Midwest. (With R. E. Wood.) *Wilson Bulletin* 80:173–188.* http://digitalcommons.unl.edu/biosciornithology/7

– A review of parental carrying of young by waterfowl. (With Janet Kear.) *The Living Bird* 7:89–102.* http://digitalcommons.unl.edu/biosciornithology/32

– Some putative mandarin duck hybrids. *Bulletin British Ornithological Club* 88:140–148.* http://digitalcommons.unl.edu/johnsgard/26

– Some observations on maccoa duck behavior. *Ostrich* 39:219–222.* http://digitalcommons.unl.edu/johnsgard/15

1969 – The masked duck in the United States. (With Dirk Hagemayer.) *Auk* 86:691–695.* http://digitalcommons.unl.edu/biosciornithology/60/

1970 – A summary of intergeneric New World quail hybrids, and a new intergeneric combination. *Condor* 72:85–88.* http://digitalcommons.unl.edu/biosciornithology/77

1971 – Experimental hybridization of the New World quail (Odontophorinae). *Auk* 88:264–275.* http://digitalcommons.unl.edu/biosciornithology/59

1972 – Observations on sound production of the Anatidae. *Wildfowl* 22:46–59.* http://digitalcommons.unl.edu/johnsgard/13

1973 – Proximate and ultimate determinations of clutch size in the Anatidae. *Wildfowl* 24:144–49.* http://digitalcommons.unl.edu/johnsgard/12

1974 – The taxonomy and relationships of the northern swans. *Wildfowl* 25:155–161.* http://digitalcommons.unl.edu/johnsgard/11

– Seventy-five years of changes in mallard–black duck ratios in eastern North America. (With Rose DiSilvestro.) *American Birds* 30:904–908.* http://digitalcommons.unl.edu/biosciornithology/58/

1977 – Sixty-five years of whooping crane records in Nebraska. (With Richard Redfield.) *Nebraska Bird Review* 45:54–56.* http://digitalcommons.unl.edu/johnsgard/9

1987 – The ornithogeography of the Great Plains states. *Prairie Naturalist* 10:97–112.* http://digitalcommons.unl.edu/johnsgard/8/

1979 – The breeding birds of Nebraska. *Nebraska Bird Review* 47:3–14.* http://digitalcommons.unl.edu/johnsgard/10

– The American wood quails (*Odontophorus*). *World Pheasant Association Journal IV*, pp. 93–99.

– *Anseriformes* section (Anatidae and Anhimidae), in *Check-list of the Birds of the World*. Cambridge: Harvard University Press, pp. 425–506.* http://digitalcommons.unl.edu/johnsgard/32

1980 – Migration schedules of nonpasserine birds in Nebraska. *Nebraska Bird Review* 48:26–36.* http://digitalcommons.unl.edu/nebbirdrev/734/

– Migration schedules of passerine birds in Nebraska. *Nebraska Bird Review* 48:46–57.* http://digitalcommons.unl.edu/nebbirdrev/739

– A revised list of the birds of Nebraska and adjoining plains states. *Occasional Publications of the Nebraska Ornithologists' Union No. 6*. 160 pp. (Reprinted and revised several times.)

1981 – Observations on the displays and relationships of the Argentine blue-billed duck (*Oxyura vittata*). (With Christi Nordeen.) *Wildfowl* 32:5–9.

1982 – Ethoecological aspects of hybridization in the Tetraonidae. *World Pheasant Association Journal VII*, pp. 42–57.

1983 – Hybridization and zoogeographic patterns in pheasants. *World Pheasant Association Journal VIII*, pp. 88–98.* http://digitalcommons.unl.edu/johnsgard/17

1984 – Birds of Lake McConaughy and the North Platte Valley, Oshkosh to Keystone. (With Richard Rosche.) *Nebraska Bird Review* 52:26–36.

1986 – The monographic literature of the Galliformes. *World Pheasant Association Journal XI*, pp. 21–28.* http://digitalcommons.unl.edu/johnsgard/18

1989 – Five chapters in *The Ruffed Grouse*, Harrisburg, PA: Stackpole. [The king of game birds, pp. 2–7; A proud pedigree, pp. 8–14; Courtship and mating, pp. 112–117; Nesting, pp. 130–137; The young grouse, pp. 140–159.]

1996 – The birds of the Cedar Point Biological Station area, Keith and Garden Counties, Nebraska: Seasonal occurrences and breeding data. (With Charles R. Brown, Mary B. Brown, Josef Kren, and William C. Scharf.) *Transactions of the Nebraska Academy of Sciences* 25:91–108.* http://digitalcommons.unl.edu/tnas/79

1997 – A George Miksch Sutton bibliography. *Nebraska Bird Review* 65:46–58.* (Addendum published 1998, *Nebraska Bird Review* 66:3, 67:1). http://digitalcommons.unl.edu/nebbirdrev/518/

1998 – A half-century of winter bird surveys at Lincoln and Scottsbluff, Nebraska. *Nebraska Bird Review* 66:74–84.* http://digitalcommons.unl.edu/nebbirdrev/38/

1998 – Endemicity and regional biodiversity in Nebraska's breeding birds. *Nebraska Bird Review* 66:115–121.* http://digitalcommons.unl.edu/biosciornithology/13/

1999 – Proceedings of the Centennial Meeting, Nebraska Ornithologists' Union, Lincoln, Nebraska, May 14–16, 1999. (Editor.) Published by the NOU, Lincoln. 76 pp.

2000 – A century of breeding birds in Nebraska. (With J. L. Canterbury.) *Nebraska Bird Review* 68:89–100.* http://digitalcommons.unl.edu/nebbirdrev/65/

2001 – A century of ornithology in Nebraska: A personal view. In *Contributions to the History of North American Ornithology*, vol. 2 (W. E. Davis and J. A. Jackson, eds.). Boston: Nuttall Ornithological Club, pp. 329–325.* http://digitalcommons.unl.edu/biosciornithology/26

– The ultraviolet birds of Nebraska. *Nebraska Bird Review* 67:103–105.* http://digitalcommons.unl.edu/biosciornithology/6

– Historic birds of Lincoln's Salt Basin and Nine-Mile Prairie. *Nebraska Bird Review* 68:132–136.* http://digitalcommons.unl.edu/nebbirdrev/30/

– Ecogeographic aspects of greater prairie-chicken leks in southeastern Nebraska. *Nebraska Bird Review* 68:179–184.* http://digitalcommons.unl.edu/biosciornithology/3

– Comments on Nebraska's falconiform and strigiform bird fauna. *Nebraska Bird Review* 69:80–84.* http://digitalcommons.unl.edu/nebbirdrev/305/

2002 – Nebraska's sandhill crane populations: Past, present, and future. *Nebraska Bird Review* 71:175–178.* http://digitalcommons.unl.edu/nebbirdrev/338/

2003 – The best birding in Lincoln. In *City Birding*. Harrisburg, PA: Stackpole, 92–102.

– Introduction to the 2nd edition of *Lewis and Clark: Pioneering Naturalists* by Paul Cutright. Lincoln: University of Nebraska Press, vii–xiii.

2004 – Birds. Topic entry for *Great Plains Encyclopedia*. (D. Wishart, ed.) Lincoln: University of Nebraska Press, 621–622.

2005 – Habitat associations of Nebraska birds. (With J. Dinan.) *Nebraska Bird Review* 73:20–25.

2006 – Recent changes in winter bird numbers in Lincoln, Nebraska. *Nebraska Bird Review* 74: 16–22.*
http://digitalcommons.unl.edu/nebbirdrev/294/

2007 – The Missouri and I. Chapter in *The Big Empty* (L. Randolph and N. Shevchuk-Murray, eds.). Lincoln: University of Nebraska Press, 110–113.

2009 – Online studies on Nebraska ornithology by P. A. Johnsgard. *Nebraska Bird Review* 77:77–79.

2014 – What are blue Ross's geese? *Nebraska Bird Review* 82:81–85.

Notes, Reviews, Encyclopedia Articles, and Popular Writings

1954 – Long-tailed jaeger collected in eastern Washington. *Murrelet* 35:31–32.* http://digitalcommons.unl.edu/biosciornithology/65/

1955 – Fall distribution of birds in a Palouse River canyon. *Ecology* 36:754–755.* http://digitalcommons.unl.edu/johnsgard/14/

1960 – Review of *A Colored Key to Waterfowl of the World*. *Auk* 76:109.* http://digitalcommons.unl.edu/biosciornithology/68

1962 – Review of Sex ratios and age ratios of North American ducks. *Auk* 79:287–288.* http://digitalcommons.unl.edu/biosciornithology/74

1965 – The elusive musk duck. *Natural History*, October, pp. 26–29. (Reprinted in *Tier*, pp. 11–13, 1966, under the title "Die Ente mit dem Plumpslaut"). http://digitalcommons.unl.edu/biosciornithology/30/

1967 – Dawn rendezvous on the lek. *Natural History*, March, pp. 16–20.

1968 – The evolution of duck courtship. *Natural History*, February, pp. 58–63.* (Reprinted in *Field Studies in Natural History*, New York: Van Nostrand Reinhold, 1970, pp. 123–129. http://digitalcommons.unl.edu/biosciornithology/31/

1969 – Review of *Waterfowl of Australia*. *Wilson Bulletin*, 81:230–231.

1970 – Articles on Goose and Swan in *Encyclopedia Americana*, 13:80–82 and 26: 89–90.

1971 – Article on Animal Behavior. *Colliers Encyclopedia* 2:214–219.

1972 – Torrent ducks of the Andes. *Animals* (London), February, pp. 80–83.* http://digitalcommons.unl.edu/johnsgard/31/

– The elusive tree quails of Mexico. *Animals* (London), November, pp. 486–490.* http://digitalcommons.unl.edu/johnsgard/30/

1973 – Social behavior of ducks. In *The Merck Veterinary Manual*, 4th ed., Rahway, NJ: Merck, pp. 1451–1453.

– How many cranes make a skyfull? *Animals* (London), December, pp. 532–539.* http://digitalcommons.unl.edu/johnsgard/33/

– Natural and unnatural selection in a wild goose. *Natural History*, December, pp. 60–69.* (Reprinted in *Annual Editions: Readings in Biology* 75/76). http://digitalcommons.unl.edu/biosciornithology/29

– Review of *Buffleheads* (Canadian Wildlife Service). *Bird-banding* 44: 242–243.

1974 – Four sections in *Raising Ducks in Captivity*, New York: Dutton. [Introduction to the duck family, pp. 17–22; Hybridization, pp. 142–146; Photographing ducks, pp. 268–272, The scientific value of waterfowl collections, pp. 273–78.]

– Review of *Curassows and Related Birds. Auk* 91:445–449.* http://digitalcommons.unl.edu/biosciornithology/78

– Waterfowl portraits. *NEBRASKAland*, November, pp. 14–21.* http://digitalcommons.unl.edu/biosciornithology/36

– Quail music: The complex calls of a bird contain clues to its evolution. *Natural History*, February, pp. 34–39. http://digitalcommons.unl.edu/biosciornithology/1/.*

– The feathered blizzard. *Wildlife* (UK), May, pp. 200–206.

1975 – The lesser snow geese of central North America. *Wildlife* 75:63–68.

1976 – Flight of the sea ducks. *Natural History*, August–September, pp. 68–73.* http://digitalcommons.unl.edu/biosciornithology/20

1978 – The triumphant trumpeters: Once reduced to a few bevies, this magnificent swan is on the road to recovery. *Natural History*, November, pp. 72–77.* http://digitalcommons.unl.edu/biosciornithology/18

1979 – Review of *Endangered Birds. Science* 203:428–429.

1980 – Where have all the curlews gone? *Natural History*, August, pp. 30–34.* http://digitalcommons.unl.edu/biosciornithology/23

– Copulatory behavior in the American bittern. *Auk* 97:868–869.*
http://digitalcommons.unl.edu/biosciornithology/57/

1981 – Review of *The Island Waterfowl* and *The Hawaiian Goose: An Experiment in Conservation. Quarterly Review of Biology* 56:85.

– The 6,000-mile odyssey of a globe-trotting bird. *American Kingdom*, June–July, pp. 17–21.

1982 – Whooper recount: A close look at these endangered cranes reveals that, while their numbers are increasing, their rate of increase is actually declining. *Natural History*, February, pp. 70–75.*
http://digitalcommons.unl.edu/biosciornithology/19

– Hummingbirds of Nebraska. *NEBRASKAland*, May, pp. 6–9.

1983 – Return and renewal. In *The Wonder of Birds*, National Geographic Society, pp. 54–106.

– The Platte: A river of birds. *Nature Conservancy News* 33(5):15.

1984 – Rare and beautiful pheasants of the world. *Zoonooz* (San Diego Zoo), 57(9):8–14.

1985 – Dabblers and divers. In Birds of Nebraska. *NEBRASKAland* 65(1):126–135.

– Buzz wings. In Birds of Nebraska. *NEBRASKAland* 65(1):80–81.*
http://digitalcommons.unl.edu/biosciornithology/34/

– Grouse. In *A Dictionary of Birds*, Berkhamstead, UK: T & A. D. Poyser, pp. 257–259.

– The aviculture and conservation of rare pheasants. *Game Bird and Conservationists' Gazette*, March 1985, pp. 37–39.

1987 – Birds of the Pribilofs. *Birder's World* 1(6):2–23.

1988 – Notes on Nebraska fauna: Common goldeneye. *NEBRASKAland* 66(7):50.

– Review of *Konza Prairie: A Tallgrass Natural History. Great Plains Quarterly* 8(4): 237–238.

– Glittering garments of the rainbow. *Birder's World* 2(4):12–16.

1989 – Social behavior of North American owls. *Terra* 27(3):6–11.*
http://digitalcommons.unl.edu/johnsgard/27

– On display. *Birder's World* 3(6):30–34.

1990 – Additional observations on the birds of the Lake McConaughy region. *Nebraska Bird Review* 58:52–54.*
http://digitalcommons.unl.edu/nebbirdrev/546

- Bustards: Stalkers of the dry plains. *Zoonooz* (San Diego Zoo), 63(7):5–11.
- First Nebraska kittiwake specimen. *Nebraska Bird Review* 58:75.* http://digitalcommons.unl.edu/nebbirdrev/555
- Survey for least terns and other birds on the North and South Platte rivers, eastern Keith County. *Nebraska Bird Review* 58:84–87.

1992 – A chorus of cranes. *Zoonooz* (San Diego Zoo), 65(5):6–11.
- Crane music. *NEBRASKAland* 70(2):8–19.

1993 – American white pelicans and double-crested cormorants. *NEBRASKA-land* 71(3):14–21.
- Happy birthday, Nebraska. In *Nebraska Voices: Telling the Stories of Our State*, Nebraska Humanities Council, Lincoln, pp. 160–161.

1995 – Daffy but dapper: A serious approach to the comical-looking ruddy duck. *Birder's World*, April 1995, pp. 48–51.* http://digitalcommons.unl.edu/biosciornithology/21/

1996 – The cranes of Nebraska. *Museum Notes* (University of Nebraska State Museum) 93:1–4.

1998. – Review of *A Guide to Nests, Eggs, and Nestlings of North America Birds. Auk* 115:818.* http://digitalcommons.unl.edu/biosciornithology/81
- In memoriam: Charles G. Sibley. *Nebraska Bird Review* 66:68–69.* http://digitalcommons.unl.edu/biosciornithology/12/
- A half-century of winter bird surveys at Lincoln and Scottsbluff, Nebraska. *Nebraska Bird Review* 66:74–84.* http://digitalcommons.unl.edu/nebbirdrev/38

1999 – Buzz-wings: The hummingbirds of Nebraska. *Museum Notes* (University of Nebraska State Museum). 4 pp.
- The captive status and breeding of rare and endangered pheasants. *Game Bird Breeders' Gazette* 45(2):4, 14–16, 19, 61.
- Marvelous, mystical tropical trogons. *The Living Bird* 18(3):18–22.* http://digitalcommons.unl.edu/biosciornithology/28
- Review of *Swallow Summer. Great Plains Quarterly* 9:201–202.* http://digitalcommons.unl.edu/greatplainsresearch/449
- The age of birds in Nebraska. *Nebraska Bird Review* 67: 37–40.* http://digitalcommons.unl.edu/biosciornithology/14

2000 – What in the world is a pheasant? *Zoonooz* (San Diego Zoo), April 2000, pp. 14–19.

– A temple of the intellect. *Nebraska Life* 5(2):39–43.

– The history of life in Nebraska. *NEBRASKAland*, December, pp. 24–27.* http://digitalcommons.unl.edu/biosciornithology/33/

– Review of *Great Texas Birds. Great Plains Research* 11:203–204.* http://digitalcommons.unl.edu/greatplainsresearch/549

– Foreword to *The Nebraska Breeding Bird Atlas* (W. Mollhoff, ed.) Lincoln: Nebraska Game and Parks Commission.

– Species accounts (18) for the Dorling Kindersley *Illustrated Encyclopedia of Animals*. London, UK: Dorling Kindersley.

– The last act of the heath hen drama. *Grouse Partnership News* 2(1):11.

– How do J. J. Audubon and John Gould rank as ornithologists and artists? 2001 catalog, Kenyon Oppenheimer, Chicago, pp. 3–4.

2002 – Nebraska's sandhill crane populations, past, present and future. *Nebraska Bird Review* 70:175–177.* http://digitalcommons.unl.edu/nebbirdrev/338

– Review of *Kansas Breeding Bird Atlas. Great Plains Research* 12: 403–404.* http://digitalcommons.unl.edu/greatplainsresearch/623

2003 – Great gathering on the Great Plains. *National Wildlife* 41(3):20–29.* http://digitalcommons.unl.edu/johnsgard/38/

– Introductory comments to John Gould's *Monograph of the Odontophoridae, or Partridges of North America*. CD produced by Linda Hall Library, Kansas City, MO.

– Birds. In *Great Plains Encyclopedia* (D. Wishart, ed.). Lincoln: University of Nebraska Press, pp. 621–622.

– Sibley's new twins: Book review. *Birder's World* 17(6)(December): 71–72.* http://digitalcommons.unl.edu/biosciornithology/22/

2004 – In explorers' footsteps: You can find nearly all the birds documented by Lewis and Clark in great refuges on the Great Plains. *Birder's World* 18(2)(April): 31–37.* http://digitalcommons.unl.edu/biosciornithology/2/

– Foreword, In *Effects of Management Practices on Grassland Birds* (D.H. Johnson, L. D. Igl, and J. A. Dechant Shaffer, series coordinators). Jamestown, ND: Northern Prairie Wildlife Research Center.

2006 – The howdy owl and the prairie dog. *Birding* 38(1):40–44.

– Review of *In the Company of Crows and Ravens. Great Plains Research* 16:217.* http://digitalcommons.unl.edu/greatplainsresearch/853

- Recent changes in winter bird numbers at Lincoln, Nebraska. *Nebraska Bird Review* 74:16–22.*
  http://digitalcommons.unl.edu/nebbirdrev/294
- A book collector's guide to Roger Tory Petersen. *Nebraska Bird Review* 74:61–63.* http://digitalcommons.unl.edu/nebbirdrev/287
- The art and artistic legacy of Louis Agassiz Fuertes. *Nebraska Bird Review* 74:132–141.* http://digitalcommons.unl.edu/nebbirdrev/83

2007 – Review of *Watchable Birds of the Black Hills, Badlands, and Northern Great Plains. Great Plains Research* 17:20.*
  http://digitalcommons.unl.edu/greatplainsresearch/876
- A dozen squaretails and a sharpy. *Nebraska Life*, March–April, pp. 80–86.
- Review of *Conservation of the Black-tailed Prairie Dog. Prairie Naturalist* 39 (3/4):200–201.

2008 – The Platte: River of dreams or river of dust? *Prairie Fire* 1(5):12–19.
  http://www.prairiefirenewspaper.com/2007/11/the-platte
- Review of *Texas Quails: Ecology and Management. Great Plains Research* 17:233.* http://digitalcommons.unl.edu/greatplainsresearch/897
- The altruistic cardinal? *Nebraska Life*, November–December, 2008.*
  http://digitalcommons.unl.edu/johnsgard/41
- Review of *John Kirk Thompson: Collector of Audubon's Western Birds and Mammals. Nebraska Bird Review* 76:84–85.
- Review of *Owls of the United States and Canada. Great Plains Research* 19:134.
- Review of *Birding in the Northern Plains: The Ornithological Writings of Herbert Krause. Nebraska Bird Review* 76:171.

2009 – Reflections on Charles Darwin and his enduring legacy. *Prairie Fire*, February, 2009, pp. 12–15. http://prairiefirenewspaper.com/2009/02/reflections-on-charles-darwin
- The wings of March. *Prairie Fire*, March 2009, pp. 1, 17, 18, 19. http://www.prairiefirenewspaper.com/2009/03/nature-notes-wings-of-march
- The oldest romance in the West. *Nebraska Life*, April 2009, pp. 64–67.*
  http://digitalcommons.unl.edu/johnsgard/42
- A hummer summer. *Bird Watchers' Digest* 31(8):34–39.
- Autumn on the prairie: Grasses of Nebraska. *Nebraska Life*, September–October, 2009, pp. 18–21.*
  http://digitalcommons.unl.edu/johnsgard/40

165

– Nebraska's 8 great natural wonders. *Nebraska Life*, November 2009, pp. 78–84.* http://digitalcommons.unl.edu/johnsgard/39/

– Forbs and grasses and Cheshire cats: What is a tallgrass prairie? *Prairie Fire*, December 2009, pp. 3, 9. http://www.prairiefirenewspaper.com/2009/12/ forbs-and-grasses-and-cheshire-cats-what-is-a-tallgrass-prairie

– Review of *Cranes: A Natural History of a Bird in Crisis. Great Plains Research* 20(1). Paper 1903.* http://digitalcommons.unl.edu/greatplainsresearch/1093/

2010 – Snow geese on the Great Plains. *Prairie Fire*, February 2010, pp. 12–15. http://www.prairiefirenewspaper.com/2010/02/ snow-geese-on-the-great-plains

– The drums of April. *Prairie Fire*, April 2010, pp. 12–13. http://www.prairiefirenewspaper.com/2010/04/the-drums-of-april

– A place called Pahaku, *Prairie Fire*, June 2010, pp. 1, 19, 20, 23. http://www.prairiefirenewspaper.com/2010/06/a-place-called-pahaku

– The peregrines of Nebraska. *Prairie Fire*, August 2010, pp. 12–14. http://www.prairiefirenewspaper.com/2010/08/ the-peregrine-falcons-of-nebraska

– The whooping cranes: Survivors against all odds. (With K. Gil-Weir.) *Prairie Fire*, September 2010, pp. 12, 13, 16, 22. http://www.prairiefire-newspaper.com/2010/08/the-peregrine-falcons-of-nebraska

2011 – Sandhill cranes: Nebraska's avian ambassadors at large. (With K. Gil-Wier.) *Prairie Fire*, March 2011, pp. 14, 15, 20. http://www.prairiefirenewspaper.com/2011/02/ sandhill-cranes-our-avian-ambassadors-at-large

– The secretive shorebirds: Nebraska's phantom migrants. *Prairie Fire*, April 2011. http://www.prairiefirenewspaper.com/2011/04/ the-secretive-shorebirds-nebraskas-phantom-migrants

– Raptors of Nebraska. *Prairie Fire*, November 2011, pp. 14–14. http:// www.prairiefirenewspaper.com/2011/11/the-raptors-of-nebraska

– The feathers of winter. *Prairie Fire*, December 2011, pp. 17–20. http://www.prairiefirenewspaper.com/2011/12/the-feathers-of-winter

2012 – Nebraska's magical sandhill crane migration. *Prairie Fire*, February 2012, pp. 1, 3, 4, 5. http://prairiefirenewspaper.com/2012/02/ nebraskas-magical-sandhill-crane-migration

– The owls of Nebraska. *Prairie Fire*, February 2012, pp. 15, 20. http://www.prairiefirenewspaper.com/2012/02/the-owls-of-nebraska

- The birds of Nebraska's boondocks. *Prairie Fire*, April 2012, pp. 8–10. http://www.prairiefirenewspaper.com/2012/04/the-birds-of-nebraskas-boondocks

- It's crane season—in Wyoming. *Prairie Fire*, June 2012, pp. 1, 3, 4. http://www.prairiefirenewspaper.com/2012/06/its-crane-season-in-wyoming

- Birds of the tallgrass prairie. *Prairie Fire*, July 2012, pp.16–19. http://www.prairiefirenewspaper.com/2012/07/birds-of-the-tallgrass-prairies

- A dazzle of hummingbirds. *Prairie Fire*, September 2012, pp. 12–13. http://www.prairiefirenewspaper.com/2012/09/a-dazzle-of-hummingbirds

- Spring Creek Prairie Audubon Center: An 800-acre schoolhouse. *Prairie Fire*, October 2012, pp. 18–20, 22. http://www.prairiefirenewspaper.com/2012/10//spring-creek-prairie-audubon-center-an-800-acre-schoolhouse

- Squaw Creek National Wildlife Refuge: Gem of the Missouri Valley. *Prairie Fire*, November 2012, pp. 12–13. http://www.prairiefirenewspaper.com/2012/11/squaw-creek-national-wildlife-refuge-gem-of-the-missouri-valley

- The eagles of Nebraska. *Prairie Fire*, December 2012, pp. 9, 14, 15, 16. http://www.prairiefirenewspaper.com/2012/12/the-eagles-of-nebraska

2013 - The swans of Nebraska. *Prairie Fire*, January 2013, pp. 12–13. http://www.prairiefirenewspaper.com/2013/01/the-swans-of-nebraska

- Nebraska bird-feeder birds: What's in your backyard? *Prairie Fire*, February 2013, pp. 2, 5, 6. http://www.prairiefirenewspaper.com/2013/02/nebraska-bird-feeder-birds-whats-in-your-backyard

- A plethora of pelicans. *Prairie Fire*, March 2013, pp. 9–11. http://www.prairiefirenewspaper.com/2013/03/a-plethora-of-pelicans

- How to shoot cranes (photographically). *Prairie Fire*, March 2013, pp. 22–23. http://www.prairiefirenewspaper.com/2013/03/how-to-shoot-cranes-photographically

- The greater prairie chicken: Spirit of the tallgrass prairie. *Prairie Fire*, April 2013, pp. 14–15. http://www.prairiefirenewspaper.com/2013/04/the-greater-prairie-chicken-spirit-of-the-tallgrass-prairie

- The grouse with the pointed tail, *Prairie Fire*, April 2013, pp. 16–18. http://www.prairiefirenewspaper.com/2013/04/.../the-grouse-with-the-pointed-tail

– A Yellowstone story. *Prairie Fire*, August 2013, pp. 1, 3, 4. http://www.prairiefirenewspaper.com/2013/08/a-yellowstone-story

– Foreword to Paothong, N., and J. M. Vance, 2012, *Save the Last Dance: A Story of the North American Grassland Grouse*, Columbia, Missouri: N. Paothong.

– Changing Great Plains climate and bird migrations. *Prairie Fire*, December 2013, pp. 1, 3, 5. http://www.prairiefirenewspaper.com/2013/12/changing-great-plains-climate-and-bird-migrations

2014 – To kill a mountain lion. *Prairie Fire*, January 2014, pp. 18–19. http://www.prairiefirenewspaper.com/2014/02/to-kill-a-mountain-lion

– The allure of cranes. *Prairie Fire*, March 2014, pp. 1, 3, 4. Reprinted in 2015 in *Natural Treasures of the Great Plains: An Ecological Perspective*.

– Great spring birding in the Great Plains. *Prairie Fire*, April 2014, pp. 14–16. http://www.prairiefirenewspaper.com/2014/04/great-spring-birding-on-the-great-plains

– Aransas National Wildlife Refuge: The whooping crane's vulnerable winter retreat. *Prairie Fire*, May 2014, pp. 12–13. http://www.prairiefirenewspaper.com/2014/05/aransas-national-wildlife-refuge-the-whooping-cranes-vulnerable-winter-retreat

– Foreword to Phillips, Jack, *The Bur Oak Manifesto: Seeking Nature and Planting Trees in the Great Plains*. Lincoln, NE: Prairie Fire Press.

– The Hutton Niobrara Ranch Audubon Nature Sanctuary. *Prairie Fire*, July 2014, pp. 12–14. http://www.prairiefirenewspaper.com/2014/07/hutton-niobrara-ranch-wildlife-sanctuary

– The lives and deaths of Yellowstone's grizzlies. *Prairie Fire*, August 2014, pp. 1–3. http://www.prairiefirenewspaper.com/2014/08/the-lives-and-deaths-of-yellowstones-grizzlies

– Secrets of the very long dead: Ashfall Fossil Beds State Historical Park. *Prairie Fire*, October 2014, pp. 1, 3, 4. http://www.prairiefirenewspaper.com/2014/10/secrets-of-the-very-long-dead-ashfall-fossil-beds-state-historical-park

2015 – Secrets of the most sincerely dead: Agate Fossil Beds National Monument. *Prairie Fire*, November 2014, pp. 15–17. http://www.prairiefirenewspaper.com/2014/11/secrets-of-the-most-sincerely-dead-agate-fossil-beds-national-monument

– Climate change and its biological effects in the Great Plains. *Prairie Fire*, April 2015, pp. 6–8.

http://www.prairiefirenewspaper.com/2015/04/
climate-change-and-its-biological-effects-in-the-great-plains
- In praise of prairie fires and the lasting legacies of the temporary. Foreword to *Natural Treasures of the Great Plains: An Ecological Perspective.* Lincoln, NE: Chronicles Press, xiii–xx.
- Nebraska: Where the West begins (and the East peters out). *Prairie Fire,* May 2015, pp. 8–9. http://www.prairiefirenewspaper.com/2015/05/
nebraska-where-the-west-begins-and-the-east-peters-out
- Grebes, godwits, and other gifts of glaciers past. *Prairie Fire,* August-September 2015 (in press).

Online Biographies and Interviews

Hayward, J. 1994. Beguiled by birds. *Living Bird* 13(4):6–7.* http://digitalcommons.unl.edu/biosciornithology/27
Scully, M. G. 2001. Heeding the call of sandhill cranes. *Chronicle of Higher Education* 47(30):B-17.* http://digitalcommons.unl.edu/johnsgard/37
Winner, C. 2006. Rare bird. *Washington State Magazine* 5(4):38–45.* http://wsm.wsu.edu/s/index.php?id=668
Curran, Jack. 2009. A profile of Dr. Paul A. Johnsgard. *Prairie Fire* 3(6)1: 18–21. http://www.prairiefirenewspaper.com/2009/06/a-profile-of-dr-paul-a-johnsgard
Johnsgard, Paul. 2010. My life in biology. *Nebraska Bird Review* 78(3): 103–120.* http://digitalcommons.unl.edu/biosciornithology/82/
Paul Johnsgard. 2012. Wikipedia [biography and selected citations]. https://en.wikipedia.org/wiki/Paul_Johnsgard

Miscellaneous Interviews and Profiles

Miles, L. 1993. Paul Johnsgard and the harmony of nature. In: A. Jenkins (ed.), *The Platte River: An Atlas of the Big Bend Region.* Kearney: University of Nebraska–Kearney, pp. 91–93.
Farrar, J. 1993. Paul Johnsgard, Nebraska's birdman. *NEBRASKAland* 71(2):38–47.
Klucas, G. 2002. A beautiful mind. *Nebraska Magazine* (Summer), 24–27.

Klucas, G. 2003. Paul Johnsgard . . . For the birds. *Nebraska Life* (September-October), 34–37.

Ducey, J. 2005. Bird man. *L Magazine* (*Lincoln* [Nebraska] *Journal Star*) (June), 38–39.

Berlowitz, D. 2008. For the birds: Education meets photography. *Living Well* (Lincoln, NE Center for Aging) 4(4):16–19.

Hendee, David. 2011. A mystical migration. *Omaha World-Herald*, April 9, D-1–2.

Hendee, David. 2013. Capturing Yellowstone: Project came naturally. *Omaha World-Herald*, August 31, A-1–2.

American Ornithologists' Union, Ralph W. Schreiber Conservation Award Citation, 2012. *Auk* 130(1):205–6.
http://www.aou.org/awards/senior/conservation/

Zea Books by Paul A. Johnsgard

At Home and at Large in the Great Plains: Essays and Memories
(2015)

Global Warming and Population Responses among Great Plains Birds
(2015)

Música de las Grullas: Una historia natural de las grullas de América,
trans. Enrique H. Weir & Karine Gil-Weir (2014)

Birds and Birding in Wyoming's Bighorn Mountains Region, by
Jacqueline Canterbury, Paul Johnsgard, & Helen Downing
(2013)

Birds of the Central Platte River Valley and Adjacent Counties, by
Mary Bomberger Brown & Paul A. Johnsgard (2013)

The Birds of Nebraska: Revised Edition, 2013 (2013)

A Prairie's Not Scary (2012)

Wings over the Great Plains: Bird Migrations in the Central Flyway
(2012)

*Wetland Birds of the Central Plains: South Dakota, Nebraska and
Kansas* (2012)

Rocky Mountain Birds (2011)

A Nebraska Bird-Finding Guide (2011)

http://www.lulu.com/spotlight/unllib

www.ingramcontent.com/pod-product-compliance
Lightning Source LLC
Chambersburg PA
CBHW021159010426
R18062100002B/R180621PG41931CBX00026B/5